Anxiety can Save You

How a book on anxiety can change your life...

Francesca Frascarelli

& Giuseppina Pollino

Acknowledgements

No one has come into my life by chance…

Every person has left something with me, every person has helped me to evolve; to understand who I am and what is good for me and for my life.

Even bad moments taught me; they taught me to choose on which side to stand. Past love and friendships are the foundation for the present ones; never deny them. Disappointment has helped me to understand when is the moment to fight and when is the moment to desist, because sometimes the only right strategy is to stop. It doesn't mean to give up but to accept, to welcome what life gives us, because sometimes, when things are not how we want it to be, it is simply because they shouldn't be how we want. Thus, great satisfactions make you understand that you were right in not sparing your energy and give all you have for what you believe in, never underestimate our successes. We need to always remember that there is always the right moment for everything. I started writing this book a year and a half ago but only now I am ready to complete it.

To whom I want to dedicate this book, to whom unfortunately didn't manage to transform fear into strength, to two people who are not here anymore but who knows, maybe also this is a part of a bigger plan: my grandma and my uncle. I think that without your experience I will not be here to do what I do.

And to my little Giusy, my inseparable friend who never ceased to motivate me with her sweet and rosy ideas to contemplate this book which, otherwise, I would probably have left incomplete.

Index

Preface

By *Giuseppina Pollino*

Everyday, we can see people committed to ruining their lives. Everyday these people complain because they want a better life, a better partner, a better job, a better world. But everyday, every single day, they protect that reassuring and masochistic form of home that they call "their everyday life". Because after all, even if it's devastating, it's something extremely familiar. Maybe this "familiarity" has been learnt from a parent or from a love story gone wrong, but from that moment it has become their script. Even if the script is wrong, they know the ending and only because they know it, they feel protected, even if it's a sad ending in an aloof scene. You can't even dare to show them that perhaps a happier world is possible; that if they fight jealousy and bigotry with trust and love, maybe their life or their relationship may be more unrestricted and a bit healthier; that maybe their work could become their passion and not their only reason to live an existence of sacrifices and complaints; that maybe if at every wake up they thank the universe for the beauty it has given to them, bad things wouldn't seem so bad compared to all the wonders in the world. But you, again, cannot dare to show all this beauty to those who don't have the mindset and even worse, the hearth open to welcome this happiness. If they are not ready they will certainly start to hate you. This is why *"Anxiety can Save You"* is a present that you should give, especially to yourself. The author has certainly taken the risk to be hated but with a noble purpose: to free people from the slavery of a life controlled by anxiety. If you have noticed the title of this book, perhaps flicked through a few pages, you are one of those people who knows that there is something wrong in that terrible sensation that attacks you everyday. Changes frighten everyone because it means to jump into the unknown and anxiety feeds from fear, it is it's favourite. The principle that Doctor Francesca Maria Frascarelli has set as the basis for her manual is to make the unknown known because this is a fundamental law of life: the more you know, the less you fear. The more you face your fear, the more it changes. Through these pages you will learn to speak the same language of your anxiety and only understanding its meaning you can answer back adequately. That is why I would say that this is a linguistic manual, practical and interpretative where, thanks to comprehension, anxiety will not be a problem for you anymore but it will become your ally, an energy that you can use as you wish in a completely new and unexpected way giving an added value to your personality. It's incredible how your life can change with 10 simple tricks. You will learn that everything you believed were an indivisible part of your character, of your weaknesses derives from specific mechanisms and, in an instant, you will be able to radically transform them into your best characteristic. Nothing will happen by magic but it will be well structured through precise physical and mental exercises collected in the manual you are about to read, currently the most comprehensive manual about anxiety on the market. Remember, the protagonist is you, anxiety is yours but from today you will learn to use it as you wish.

Introduction

Anxiety grows without control and the more we try to control it, the more it flees. I have already seen too many people ruin their life, sometimes getting sick, with their own hands, or rather, with their thoughts and, every time this happens, I feel a terrible disappointment and anger. I don't want to feel this way anymore or at least I want to try to do everything I can to avoid that awful sensation of 'powerlessness'. Now that I know how things work, I cannot allow them to remain like this, I don't really like the outcome too often. The solution to our distress is easier than the one you are looking for. We are going toward a wrong direction, this is the reality. The body knows what is the best for it, it has wisdom and intelligence and when it feels that system doesn't work anymore, it makes us understand it through its instruments: the symptoms. At this point I am more and more convinced that everything has a sense, a precise meaning that invades a precise period of our life. I think it's no use to get lost into a long and complicated reasoning, now it's time to act. But first, we need to unlearn and then create a new and more solid basis. This is the reason that pushed me to write this book, I want to share all my knowledge to help you to stop this unhealthy mechanism that hinders you to go on, that prevents you enjoying your full potential, that is ruining your life. I may seem presumptuous, ambitious, and for most sceptics; a little megalomaniac but I think this book may be the starting point for a series of changes that will save your life. I warn you, much will depend on you. I put everything I have, now it's your turn. You must assure me that you too will put everything you have and you will not give up at the first hurdle because I can guarantee you that there will be many difficulties in this path. Remember that the aim of this book is not to read it to know more about the topic or because it seems interesting, this book is born with the very precise purpose to help you to act and change immediately your way of living. Thus, if you are not willing to act it is useless to start reading it. But I will now anticipate how the book is structured. In the first chapter I will reveal you the profound truths about anxiety so that you can begin to understand the reason why it comes knocking on your door every so often. Anxiety has a message for you. In the second chapter, on the other hand, I will explain to you how anxiety strengthened itself over time and what are the mechanisms that nourish it, or rather the self –perpetuating mechanism.

I will show you in detail how it works, what are the mistakes you make without even noticing and how all of this generates anxiety. In the third chapter, I will begin to propose practical exercises to free you from anxiety by acting upon your body. You will understand that acting upon your body is a quick way to regain your emotional stability and unlock the vital energy that you have but keep somewhere in your body. The third chapter instead is configured as a real training in view of the last part of the book. In the fourth chapter written by Dr. Giuseppina Pollino, psychologist and sexologist, we will continue to focus on the body but this time on sex. Anxiety pervades every aspect of your life and certainly sex is no exception. The innovative aspect of this aspect, let me tell you, is the program to get rid of performance anxiety in 3 weeks and, even if you do not suffer from performance anxiety, the program will be very helpful to improve your sexual life. In the fifth chapter you will have very detailed guidelines to live without anxiety and to prevent it, the game, as you will know from the reading, is to always keep "your" perfect equilibrium, so that anxiety cannot find fertile ground. I will focus on the importance of being able to sleep in a truly restful way, knowing how to nourish our brain, how to take the right supplements and lastly, on physical activity, an indispensable ingredient to live well but, above all to alleviate the symptoms of anxiety. Using sports as "catharsis", which will able to free us from the toxins stored in the body. All this knowledge is thanks to behavioural techniques studied ad hoc and applicable with excellent results from everyone. And then finally get to the sixth chapter which is the most practical part in absolute, in which I will outline the 21 most effective techniques to finally free yourself from anxiety and to live the life you want. This last part is a real operative manual to be always consulted in this first phase of change and then use it only in the moment of doubt or uncertainty; in order to find the solutions you are looking for. A sort of compass to help find the way and always carry with you. Before starting, always remember that there is only one way to see the results and it is to act.

Chapter 1

Know the anxiety: the energy that changes your life

1.1 Why does anxiety come?

What I'm about to tell you is the story of how anxiety transforms from a dreaded enemy into becoming your most intimate ally. I do not want to immediately explain what it is and how it manifests itself from the physiological point of view, my first objective is to clarify its real meaning. Just by understanding it, you can save yourself! Just by understanding what it tells you is helpful. All the rest is useless chatter of professionals. You have great luck and you don't know it yet. You don't know that in a few weeks you will thank anxiety. It will seem paradoxical but if the anxiety did not come knocking at your door, you would have continued to live an unauthentic life. A brain life, fake and banal. Far from your nature. Far from your centre. A life that doesn't excites you. You would have continued to live a non-ideal life. Do you think that is madness? Fortunately, however, something in you rebelled, something was deeply tired, fed up and it came out.

"All our discomfort is nothing but the unheard voice of the soul that wants us to find our uniqueness, our way, our destiny."

Anxiety is the fear of losing everything in a second; it is the whole life that we have not lived and that we cannot live, it is the representation of the fear of losing, of always wanting to put yourself in the right place at the right time, of always knowing what to do and how to do it.

"It is the syndrome of doing in which one loses it's being."

Do everything in the right way as you should do, just as it was imposed, to not disappoint anyone, to not be judged negatively and, above all, to avoid the sense of guilt.

Do, do, do, losing our identities completely. Very sad, isn't it? But all of this has a price and so, fortunately at some point in your life, anxiety suddenly breaks in and tells you:

"Halt, stop for a moment, stop acting and start living."

Whether it is constant or disruptive, it warns you that you are wasting your life, that you are going in the wrong direction and, above all, that there is no sense in what you are doing, that you are neither useful nor necessary if you live only in your head. And when anxiety comes to your life, you should thank it because it is helping you to understand, to think and to question the meaning of your existence.

Even if the first reaction you had was to try to push it away, like an enemy, it didn't help. You do not have to fight it. This is not the way to deal with it. If you do, it will come back and you will drive it away again and it will only return, and this time it will be when you least expect it, most likely when you think you have escaped the danger indeed.

You are wondering, "Why?". It's simple: it's the only way to make you understand that you have a vital energy that wants to start living again. Anxiety is your alarm bell which is necessary to save you. It is not something to be avoided or defeated, it doesn't come from the outside, it is yours and it has a message for you. Anxiety wants to help you to find yourself, to live according to your natural inclination.

It is your inner voice that is refusing to submit to control and fiction.

It is the light that shows the direction.

It is the desire to love that you have put aside.

It is the desire to excel in all that you are holding back.

It's the desire to leave.

It's the desire to send everyone to hell.

It is the desire to live, to dare and to risk.

It's the desire to tell the world who you are.

It's the desire to feel alive, fully yourself.

It is the desire to START AGAIN.

It reminds you that we do not live neither to control ourselves, nor to be tested or even to meet the expectations of others. It warns you that even if you do not accept this truth; you will always live in the dimension of fatigue, effort, sense of duty, overloading yourself with responsibilities that do not belong to you and you will enter in a vortex where you will no longer see the way out, where you will forget that it was you who made this life so unbearable. That's right, anxiety speaks to you and can give you a wealth of messages and advice which are necessary to achieve your happiness.

Did you really think it was just a useless nuisance?

1.2 Why me?

Why do I suffer from anxiety? Why do I feel tense, anxious, dissatisfied more and more often?

There is only one reason: our spirit is not expressing itself, it is not working, it is not doing its job. It is the normality that kills it. Enough with the same rhetoric that external events have marked our life. We are all deeply convinced that we are like this because our history has made us like this. This narrow vision of existence makes us forget that in every individual there is something precious and special, a sort of timeless, unique energy that distinguishes us from one another. And although this is beautiful, we do nothing but drive away and reject everything that is unknown and uncertain. We have become too mental, but we are not just a brain, there is a body that speaks and is very angry with you. It is tired of your lifestyle too logical and practical. It is fed up with your reasoning, planning and attainments. This inflexibility leaves no room for the discovery of other mysterious, archaic, instinctive areas of your personality in which emotions dominate and not the tyranny of the rules you have imposed to yourself.

It's time to ask yourself:

"How far am I from my centre?"

"Where has the journey of life brought me?"

"If I'm feeling so bad, am I still in touch with the real me?"

Let's begin to look away from what we believe to know, to get rid of the past, of the causes we have chosen to explain how we are.

It is time to go back to the origins, to go home, and to do this, the causes don't count, there are no explanations nor reasoning.
First and foremost we need to awake the child within us. The solution of our uneasiness always begins with a "discovery", with the "awakening of the lost Self", which is not made up of reasoning and explanations, but of images and creativity. When we begin to see our discomforts as messengers that break into our life, we are already rediscovering ourselves. To welcome, to discern, to realize the presence of our discomforts is the first step to rediscovering ourselves.

Anxiety, panic, sadness and loneliness come from the unknown being within us and as such, they should be respected, observed and looked after. Stop being a detective who investigates and discovers the faults, you don't need them, you must go further, beyond explanation.

"Our discomforts are the waves of the sea of our authenticity: a panic attack has much more to teach us than the explanations we give to it".

Explanations and interpretations do not heal, but the surrender and the lost images DO. Working on ourselves means checking what we do not like about our souls and so we become fake and artificial. An authentic psychology does not necessarily seek the "why" of the inconveniences that come to us, but relies on the deep and primordial forces that animate our souls and then transform them into the most precious gifts we have. Those who live only with their minds end up becoming banal, normal, "like everyone else". When we use the term "normality" we refer only to a statistical standard, what most people do, but like a t-shirt or a pair of shoes, even our lives are not all the same size. Don't you think it is an absurdity to pretend that everybody wears or aspire to wear the same life, forgetting about our singular individuality? We do not suffer from anxiety but from a damned illness called "uniformity".

We constantly say that our life must remain within certain "limits" dictated by the family, the society and culture, that we should not ask questions, much less listen to the answers, but above all, we must not allow the emotions to move us and nothing painful can get close to us. So here comes the panic, and thank goodness, a wave of energy that sweeps away all the fake, the perfection and the emptiness we have built around ourselves to avoid being just who we are.

Do you think it's a coincidence that the word "panic" comes from Pan, the Greek God of nature and transgression? Do you think it's a coincidence that just when we push our luck too much, Pan comes to us and make us take off that mask, as beautiful and as fake, that is suffocating us? I don't think so. I also believe that if you are still here and continue to read these pages, you will feel that all this reflects you and you have a very deep need to change.

1.3 Why can't I control myself?

How many times do you feel there is something wrong within you? How many times have we told ourselves not to say some things and punctually we have done it? How many times, even though we know that by behaving in that way we will cause a break up, we can't hold back? In other words, how many times do we aim to be perfect and punctually fail?
And then when these intentions fail, we feel inadequate, wrong, we blame ourselves and again, we return to propose new models, new things to say or do. All this hurts us, it bothers us, even if we often don't realize it in the slightest. Guilty consciences really hurt, they hurt so much.

From today something must change. From today we promise to stop mulling over "why" we behaved like that and how we can recover, and we start to tell something different, something that sounds like this:

> *"Ok ... I didn't like myself tonight, I said things that I shouldn't have said ... well ... I'm just like this. I'm this person".*

This is the first truth: within us there is an impulse that wants to get out there, there is a side of us that is trying to express itself, an engine that drives us to call into question our "balances".

It's an unknown energy which is not wrong, that has a very specific goal in mind.
It's that internal power that knows much more about us than what we think we know.
It is that part of us that we have suffocated, it is that fresh and genuine way of being that still wants to live.
It is that child who claims his rights, he is telling us that we must stop pretending to appear strong and perfect and that we must no longer ignore what we feel.
It asks us not to play and not to pretend anymore.

It shows us that within us there is a fragility and a weakness that belongs only to us. It's us; the more we suppress it, the more we feel bad.

We want to look different and try to be the way that is liked by others, not realizing that we are always fighting, and that this fight will become hell because the more we struggle, the more we will go against ourselves.

Many of us have the idea that everything we obtain must be the result of a great effort, an immense effort.

Nothing can be so wrong:

"Success and happiness depend on having followed one's nature, and not by having yielded to compromises".

When we do what we like, we do not feel the effort. If we feel it, it means that what we are doing is not in harmony with us. Life is not a hard struggle and we must not fight against our nature.

What to do? Let's stop judging us, asking ourselves if we are doing well or poorly, telling us that tomorrow we will change, that we will not make the same mistakes and that we will start to listen to ourselves. If we listen to ourselves, we accept our weakness, we do not avoid it anymore, we do not challenge it anymore, we simply accept it. By accepting it, the relationship we have with ourselves changes and consequently the others will also change, they will begin to respect us and to esteem us because they will see our authenticity. The world will no longer be judging, we will not have to prove anything anymore because we have won the most important challenge: facing the unknown part of us and learning to respect it.

We are aware that the worst enemy of the soul is to lose spontaneity and that the soul doesn't want us to become better, more beautiful, more perfect but it only wants us to be more real. When we feel bad it's because we got it into our head that we should be someone who we aren't, and the soul takes us elsewhere. When we no longer want to follow all the good intentions that we have set for ourselves, we are finally improving and the discomfort and insecurity we have experienced will be nothing but a stepping stone for our future explosion. The more you accept the suffering, looking at it, listening to it, touching it, the more the fear disappears, and you know why? It's very simple, it is as if you took away his food: the refusal. Suffering, anxiety, panic, all feed from your avoidance, your refusal. When you neutralize this mechanism, the fear no longer has the nourishment and has no other choice than to leave, to disappear.

1.4 What does it want from me?

The heart that beats like crazy, the pain in the gut, the difficulty in digesting, and the laboured breathing are nothing but messages of protest. It is your soul that through anxiety screams:

"NO! NO! and again, NO!"

The soul wants to be heard, wants to protest against the constraints you've given yourself, the feeling of oppression you have, the warm desire you're holding back.

And now that you know what's the true meaning behind the anxiety you feel, you have to take another step forward. Now is the time to understand that there is no need to fight it, now you should give in to it. In order to live, you need to start telling yourself that you do not expect anything from yourself, you need to accept that sometimes you can do things as you can do and not as they should be done. That you are good as you are, that you love yourself even if you are not perfect. You must also know that there is nobody who loves you for the performance you provide.

Learn not to judge yourself, not to ask yourself whether you have done it well or not, learning not to give yourself a grade anymore. Only if you accept that you are completely authentic, in the 'here and now' with your doubts and uncertainties, that you are not trying to become what you have in mind or even worse, what you think others have in mind for you. Only in this way you will start to listen to your desires, your needs, your talents and only at this point you will feel at peace with yourself and with the world around you.

Stress, weariness, and frustration will disappear. Not because your future will always be peachy, but because having found yourself, will give you the certainties that will guide you in the life you have chosen to live. You will rediscover the passion, the eros and the pleasure that you had sacrificed to trap yourself in your patterns and inflexibility, only then you can say "thank you" to your body. Anxiety will allow you to breathe again! When anxiety, panic, depression and psychosomatic problems come, you just have to ask yourself:

"Which deep layer of myself do I want to bring to light?"

To recover you must, and this is the only real duty that you have, change the way you see the world: become more curious, more uncertain, learn to follow your intuition, to hear less and less the opinion of others and trust more and more the messages of your body. This will be one of your goals and how to do this, we will find out together. You will become increasingly wiser, of that wisdom that does not come from rational knowledge, but simply from respecting what you feel and what you are. You must do it! Trusting your soul is the only way to really feel good.

"In every moment of your life remember that behind the troubles and the discomforts, there is always innate knowledge".

When we suffer, that uneasiness is needed to recover our original being, it will be an opportunity to open the door to a new image, to make you discover a passion, an interest, a journey, and a life.

1.5. Is there a way out?

What would you think if I told you that everything you know about anxiety is wrong? That it did not take years and years of treatment? That it is even possible to fight anxiety alone?

Now is the time to unveil some small truths about anxiety:

1) **Anxiety is vital energy.** Anxiety is not a monster but the expression of our most vital part. The real problem is that you're holding it imprisoned, caged in a series of models, rules, behaviours that are not yours.
2) **Anxiety is the vital energy that turns against everything you're suppressing**. Try to wipe out all this fiction, break the bars of the cage you've built. It is a healthy rebellion that pushes you to find pleasure again.
3) **Anxiety is not just mental**. We are used to thinking that anxiety, depression, anger, fury and fear all depend "on our head". That is, they are purely psychological facts. But today we know very well that they are also connected to the physiology of our brain.

We have talked a lot about the first two points, now it's time to explain the third. When I say that anxiety is not just mental, I mean that even the real physical models of our brain have an enormous impact on our way of thinking, feeling and behaving. Therefore, it is true that our behaviour derives from past experiences, from the education received, from the environmental conditioning and from the stress we experience, but we also know that our cerebral physiology plays a fundamental role.

But the good news is that today we have proof that it is possible to change the physiology of our precious brain. And this means that changing your brain, or rather, it's physiology, anxiety will go away.

In the last chapter you will have more than 20 techniques for the care and optimization of the brain areas involved in anxiety, so that you can finally be free. Specifically, you will learn how to optimize the physical functioning of your brain with targeted psychological exercises. But first you should know that there is an area of your brain called *basal ganglia* which are the cause of your anxiety. These are large clusters of nerve cells working together and located deep within the brain. Basically, this area works excessively, or rather, it is you who make it work too much and when it is overactive, there the feelings of anxiety, panic, fear, tension and a tendency to worry about everything come. If your basal ganglia are hyperactive you will be particularly vulnerable to anxiety, more easily attacked by stressful situations and you will have a greater tendency to stiffen or immobilize yourself in thoughts and actions. If on the contrary your basal ganglia are hypoactive, you will have problems of concentration, motivation and dynamism.

What I want you to understand is that your anxiety, however annoying it may be, is nothing but an excess of energy resulting from an increased activity of the basal ganglia. But this also means that you have a great power, a natural explosive charge that if appropriately channelled, it can lead to huge personal and professional successes. Now this energy is caged or, at most, channelled into thoughts and activities that do not express your essence. This excess of energy could lead you to work too hard, to not accept mistakes, let alone enjoy breaks and weekends. It could happen that you may spend the day doing a thousand things, and then, on weekends, on vacation and during unorganized periods, you feel restless, anxious or weak. It is not a coincidence that many of the most decision-makers and charismatic people in the world, those who lead the largest companies, are able to do so thanks to the intense activity of their basal ganglia, which force them to work for long periods of time and feel "tireless".

Relaxing is a foreign and negative concept for you, even if you extremely need it.

You're wondering *"Ok, but what can I do?"* It's easy. In this book you will learn not only to find who you really are and to free yourself from the burden you are bearing right now, but also to exploit this excess of energy, this increase of activity in the form of motivation, to finally achieve all you want, live the life you deserve without the risk of getting stuck with anxiety.

In conclusion, we said that the basal ganglia are overactive in your brain. But we have also said that this hyperactivity is a great resource for you as long as you learn, and I'm here to help you, to control it.

"Every great resource, if brought to its excess becomes limit:
The "+""becomes "-".

This is why it is crucial to learn ways to calm the basal ganglia, to reduce anxiety, and take advantage of the overactivation of the basal ganglia, by creating the type of life we desire.

The optimal result to be achieved is:

- - anxiety
- - pressure
- - overload
- + motivation
- + recovery
- + reflection

The challenge therefore lies, once again, in finding the right balance.
I'm ready, are you?

Chapter 2

Understanding anxiety: the first step to change

2.1 If only I could stop thinking ...

I am very young but I have already seen many people ruin their lives, getting sick until they die by their own hands, or rather, with their own thoughts. Many of you will think that I am exaggerating, it's just "thoughts" after all, and here is the first big deception. Perhaps you still don't know that our mind does not distinguish imagination and reality, for our mind a thought is real. What we think is translated instantly and, unfortunately, involuntarily into emotions that in turn determine bodily and visceral changes. In the same way, the emotions that we produce define our thoughts and then, again, our behaviour.

We have always been taught of the existence of a clear distinction between body and mind, the famous *Cartesian dualism, res cogitans* and *res extensa*. In reality; the mind / body distinction is only an invention, it is fictitious, the truth is that mind and body are the same thing. But despite the more and more frequent research that shows how our thoughts and emotions have a role in determining the quality of our life (neuroscientists are creating more and more sophisticated studies every day), it doesn't seem too interesting. We prefer to care about what, when and how much to eat or play sports until it becomes an obsession, and let our minds wander. Yes, they are only thoughts, but it's no big deal. It's too bad we only eat three times a day on average but we are in touch with our thoughts 24 hours a day. It is good to get it into our mind that we are first and foremost, *mental* beings and we can allow ourselves the luxury of saying that thoughts and emotions are not our business.

Did you know that every thought you have sends electrical signals through the brain?

Thoughts have physical properties, they are real and have a considerable influence on every cell in our body. If the mind is invaded by negative

thoughts, our body, and in particular, the limbic system (the system in which the emotions are handled), will be influenced and will cause anxiety, irritability, depression, even resulting in having real physical illnesses. To free yourself from anxiety you must know and be able to change your thoughts.
Understanding how it works is the first step.

Your thought processes are characterized by a certain content, style and structure. And, even if you don't realize it, they can turn out to be irrational and dysfunctional, leading you to emotions and behaviours you do not want.

Let's take some dysfunctional examples:

1. "I need this job to be done **perfectly**"

2. "I have to do this alone or it will not be done in the **right way**"

3. "I **don't have to** waste time with these stupid things"

4. "It's better to think long before deciding or I may **be wrong**"

5. "This person's behaviour is bad and must be **punished**"

6. "It's better to **check** again to be sure it's right"

7. "I **should** have fun at this party"

These automatic thoughts are born from 7 basic assumptions that take the trouble to suggest to us how life works. Let's see them together.

1. **"There are right and wrong behaviours, decisions and emotions"**. Only a small series of actions and feelings are considered perfectly acceptable for you. Anything that does not fall within this limited field is imperfect and therefore "wrong". I'll give you another example: you could complain about your "loss of balance" because of the irritation you have felt for having invited a friend who has messed up your room whilst you hosted her. Even if your irritation can be considered largely justified, you feel annoyed by the fact that you have experienced negative emotions.

2. **"I must avoid making mistakes to be worthy of value".** When you try something or do something imperfect, you conclude that you are not good, therefore you are worthless. So, given the impossibility of being perfect, this attitude can expose you to suffer from low self-esteem and avoid certain situations. Avoiding, in turn, leads you to feel even more inadequate and frustrated. For example, you could forgo a project because you don't feel good enough.

3. **"To make a mistake means to fail" and "failure is intolerable".** The idea you have of success requires extreme perfection and this way of thinking makes the experience of failure inevitable. The fact that for you the failure is a terrible thing makes the whole thing even worse. This load of expectations means that the number of errors or faults (which are in fact, absolutely normal) are intolerable for you and a source of frustration. Here's an example: you could buy a gift for your partner but you are anguished by the idea of not knowing if they would like the gift, you think obsessively about having made a mistake and in response you avoid giving it. Just thinking that they might not like it, blocks the action and makes you anxious.

4. **"To make a mistake means deserving criticism".** The reasoning is as follows: I will inevitably be wrong and I will feel guilty. If I am not critical of myself, I will commit more errors and therefore failures. Let's say you want to start a diet and that you indulge once in a piece of cake not provided for by the menu. All this will result in your mind as lack of control and failure. You are convinced that your sense of guilt is necessary

for your balance while on the contrary, without guilt you would be unrestrained.

5. "I need to have everything under my complete control. Losing control is dangerous". This thought explains why uncertainty and accidents are so intolerable for you. Without the predictability of the world you could not maintain the complete control and avoid mistakes. That's why you're terrified of changes.

6. "If it's not safe, it's better not do anything". When there is so much uncertainty in life, the best choice is to do nothing. The prospect of failure is much less tolerable than a non-ideal life. It's better a certain unhappiness than an uncertain happiness.

7. "Without my rules and rituals I am lost". Changing or abandoning some rules or rituals is devastating. Never change a winning team.

Is it enough or should I go further? Aren't you asking a little too much from yourself? Is it not the case to be a little softer?

To worsen the picture, there are also the cognitive distortions, that is, those faulty psychological processes that lead you to a dysfunctional interpretation of the events that happen and make them fit into your model. Let's say it out loud: you march to the beat of your own drum.

1. Dichotomous thinking: it's the tendency to consider things as "everything" or "nothing" and according to a strictly "black" or "white" vision. This tendency is subject to rigidity, procrastination and perfectionism. Without this primitive and global thinking, you would see the shades of grey. You would find that things can be perfect, excellent, very good, good, fair, bad, very bad or extremely bad. According to dichotomous thinking, an imperfect but still very good decision is a wrong decision.

2. Exaltation or catastrophizing: the importance or the consequences of a mistake become greatly exaggerated. You tend to amplify the real importance of things.

3. Tyranny of the 'I must': you think and communicate in terms of "I must". The punitive, absolutist and moralistic style gives to your life the strength of the imperative and replaces the personal will with pressure as a source of personal motivation. And of course, when you cannot do what you expected yourself to do, you feel guilty and criticize yourself. If it's other people who are not doing what they should, they deserve punishment and condemnation.

Perfectionism, inflexibility, the continuous reliance on "I should" or "I must", the constant question of whether we did well or not, makes you vulnerable and it's just when you feel that life is out of your control and that the usual mechanisms do not work anymore, then at this point anxiety knocks on your door.

2.2 If only I could stop worrying ...

Edgar Cayce said:

"Thoughts are things, and as their currents run they may become crimes or miracles"

And he was right.

Our mental state has a certain colour or taste that depends on the kind of thoughts we make, which are translated into an emotional physiological state and this will inevitably have repercussions on our relationships. Therefore, we must be extremely attentive to our thoughts and always remember that we are first and foremost all mental beings, nothing is more predominant than our thoughts and that they have the power to make our lives extraordinary or dramatic, it depends only on them and therefore, it all depends only on us! Yet, there are people who still believe in genetics, in luck, in misfortune and in destiny. Here, too, is a matter of choice, let's just leave those who believe that they cannot do anything of their lives to their de-powering beliefs and let's focus on what we can do to make our lives exciting.

In this regard it is right to mention the research of the cell biologist Bruce Lipton, who made a surprising discovery on the biological mechanisms through which cells receive and process information: our genes, in fact, are controlled by us rather than control ourselves. In other words, they are under the control of environmental influences outside the cells, thoughts and beliefs included. This proves that we are not *genetic automata* victimized by the biological heritage of our ancestors. We are instead the co-creators of our life and our biology. Lipton describes this new science, called epigenetics, in the book "*The Biology of Belief*" that I invite you to read. It's really stimulating, perhaps the most beautiful book I've ever read, in which he confirms that we have immense power.

The reason why I want you to work on your negative automatic thoughts, the NAT, will now be clear.

What are NAT? Cynical, negative and painful thoughts that seem to be self-generated without our control. They are dangerous because they are rooted in our subconscious and they are even able to limit and weaken our best intentions. NAT can create bad mood and fatalism. Here is an example:

"*I already know that I will not pass the exam on Tuesday.*"

This kind of thinking is like a self-fulfilling prophecy: if someone has already convinced themself that they will not pass the exam, they will probably not study enough and consequently will not pass it. . Those who are always sad and depressed will not expect good things to happen, so they will not try hard enough to make them happen. The inner anguish caused by negative thoughts determines our attitude which will alienate others from us, causing further isolation and negativity. On the contrary, positive thoughts and attitudes will help us to spread a sense of wellbeing which is authentic that make it easier for others to get in touch with us.

"WHAT CROSSES YOUR MIND DURING THE DAY DETERMINES WHETHER YOU HAVE ADVANTAGEOUS OR COUNTER-PRODUCTIVE BEHAVIOUR"

Unfortunately, no one has taught us to give importance to our thoughts or to question the ideas that constantly cross our mind. Few people understand how important thoughts are, so the development of healthy thought patterns is left completely to chance.

And now let's see together which are the 9 most frequent and most harmful NAT. For now your task will be to identify them every time you put them into practice:

1 Think in terms of always / never: thinking using words like "always, never, nobody, everyone, everything".

2 Focus on the negative: see only the negative side of each situation.

3 Make negative predictions: always predict the worst of each situation.

4 Mind reading: to believe that you know what others think, even if they have not said it yet.

5 Thinking with feelings: blindly believing in feelings without ever questioning them.

6 Blame oneself: thinking using words like "I must, I should, I'll have to"

7 Labelling: applying a negative label to yourself or others.

8 Personalizing: give a personal meaning to harmless events.

9 Shift blame: blame others for our problems.

Here, these are the NAT, the most frequent Automatic Negative Thoughts, and, now that you know them and you know how much they are hindering your life, follow my advice: stay away from them.

 Anxiety-free love ...

Relationships are the most important thing we have. We cannot imagine a life without other people, it would be empty and we would not have anyone with who we could share joys and sorrows and for this very reason, we must cultivate them but also, we must spend time to understand which direction they are going. This is even more necessary in one-on-one relationships, in which we must become very skilled at being able to recognize the signals and the dynamics that can hinder a serene and sincere love life, provoking strong dissatisfaction. Anxiety and NAT invade the relationship, fuelling a state of never ending concern and alarmism within the couple.

For example:

"I'm worried about you"
"Let me know who you are with and where you go"
"Where are you? With who? Be careful"
"Call me otherwise I can't sleep"
"I would like that you don't go, I don't want to worry"
"Be careful with those people, I don't trust them, I have a bad feeling about them"
"Don't go, don't do it, don't look for trouble"
To conclude with the classic "I told you so, but you didn't listen to me"

If it is true that these recommendations can be read as "care", reassuring the partner to be important, when they become exaggerated and persistent they can damage the relationship to the point of breaking it. It happens in those couples where apprehension becomes the only way to express love and affection, the implicit message is:

"I show you that I love you because I worry about you".

A vicious circle is established, in which the pleasure of living the love story is lacking, because only the negative or uncertain aspects of every idea, experience, and the NAT, are taken into consideration. This atmosphere ends up pervading every aspect of the couple, sometimes compromising even the intimate life. It blocks the free expression of the other, the growth and action for fear of receiving a reproach. We stop imagining, dreaming and acting, we become increasingly gloomy, focused on preventing accidents or possible obstacles. Thoughts and behaviours are increasingly repetitive and monotonous. It's typical of the worried couple. Although concern is an integral part of our existence as it warns us about possible dangers and makes us ready to give adequate reaction, when worrying becomes a way of life, we must start worrying about our concern. Worrying triggers neuronal and hormonal mechanisms of reaction to the danger that inhibit every other impulse, including sexual impulse. For these people it is truly difficult to feel safe, to trust others, to be able to abandon themselves and not think. Living in a state of constant worry is risky for health as well as the lack of pleasure that is given to our own life. The attraction slowly fades as predictability and the feeling of imminent threat leads to put sex in the last priority.

1st rule in love:

1. Freedom is a higher value than love. So, if love destroys freedom, it has no value. When you depend on or try to control the other, he/she will certainly dominate you, and you will try to dominate the other. This is a struggle, it's not love. How can you think of dominating someone you love? You would like to see him/her totally free, independent; you would like to give him/her more individuality. In true love, individualities are not cancelled, they are strengthened. Freedom has enriched them both. Immature people who fall in love destroy one another's freedom, create a bond, a prison. Mature people in love help themselves to be free. When love flows into freedom there is beauty. When love flows into addiction there is ugliness. Remember, freedom is a higher value than love.   ; freedom must be saved: it is a higher value. Without freedom you can never be happy, it is not possible. Practice and experience first-hand the freedom in small everyday things and check the consequences. You will realize that when you start loosening your control, your partner again begins to "see you", he/she realizes that there is another part of you in addition to the control, generally it is the part they fell in love with. But above all you realize that your attitude as a controller is only worsening things, nullifying the eros and passion. Letting people to be free to live is the solution.

2.3 If only I was not such a perfectionist ...

The desire for success is part of our nature. Many of us are driven towards ever higher goals. However, to live a life that is both successful and fulfilling, our standards must be realistic and above all, we must be able to enjoy the results obtained, feeling a sense of gratitude.

"WE MUST SECURE DREAMS TO REALITY AND APPRECIATE OUR ACCOMPLISHMENTS"

What lies behind this craving for perfectionism?

-Rejection of failure
-Rejection of painful emotions
-Rejection of success

The fear of failure, in particular, can manifest itself in ceasing to experiment, thus reducing the possibility of learning, growing and in playing for time because we are frightened by undertaking a project if we are not sure of a perfect result. In playing for time, frightened by undertaking a project if we are not sure of a perfect result. Sometimes we end up turning this deep fear of failure inwards. I refer to those people who are always happy even when faced with disappointments. Inexorably optimistic people seem to immediately recover, looking unharmed from an emotional point of view, even if they live real traumas and tragedies. It is true that a positive attitude and a good capacity of recovery contribute to maintain a state of well-being, but the fact of rejecting painful emotions is unhealthy in the long run. It hides the fear of leaving space for negative emotions as if there is no space in the idealized vision of a happy and perfect life. Making detours to avoid feelings and using emotional shortcuts, this can paradoxically reduce happiness. It is easy to understand how perfectionism can lead to the rejection of failure and painful emotions. However, the surprising thing is how it can lead to the rejection of success itself. The surprising thing, however, is how it can lead to the rejection of success itself. It is the attitude that we observe in those who seem to have everything, but despite it, they are unhappy. If the only dream that we cultivate is that of a perfect life, we are destined to disappointment because the expectation controlled and created with the smallest details clashes with the unpredictability of life, continuously throwing us in front of situations that are not exactly as we "expected".

In the real world these kinds of dreams do not come true. To aspire to a perfect life can lead to great frustrations and unhappiness.

Living without perfectionism

I must also acknowledge your merits. You are an incurable perfectionist and sometimes this attitude can be extremely profitable, it leads you to work hard and to establish ever higher personal standards. The problem comes when you do not accept reality. The real problem lies in the concept of "limit". Aiming high, aiming for the best life possible is extremely different from aspiring to live "a perfect life". This is exactly the transition that the perfectionist must do to save himself. You must go from a perfectionist perspective to an "Optimalist" one. The fundamental difference lies in the fact that the perfectionist refuses the limits of reality while the optimalist accepts them, acquiring therefore a competitive advantage over the former. Maybe the perfectionist sets higher standards but he pretends that the path to his goal is free from obstacles, direct and easy. And when things do not go as he established, as it's inevitable, he will feel extremely frustrated, nervous and will have difficulty coping with the situation. He expects that reality is free from adversity. This vision, once let down, can block him, lead him to change plans or to blow everything up. Difficulties are not contemplated in the perfectionist's project. Unfortunately, reality is not always as linear.

The optimalist on the other hand, accepts failures and difficulties as experiences inextricably linked to success. He understands that the impossibility of immediately getting the job he wanted or the fact of arguing with his spouse is part of a full and fulfilling life, he learns from experience and becomes stronger and able to overcome adversities. He too aims for the best, but he wisely accepts that failure or difficulties are a necessary part of learning and life. The same attitude applies to emotions.

The perfectionist, in fact, is convinced that a happy existence is constituted by an uninterrupted series of positive emotions and therefore, he rejects the painful emotions. "Everything must go as planned". No time is left for sadness when he loses a job opportunity or experiences the profound sorrow that follows the end of an important relationship. In his code, it is impossible to cry, to talk about the disappointments, to regret, to feel sorry and to be disappointed. He faces all the adversities with extreme speed, pragmatism and coldness, he denies emotions. The surface is perfect but inside something burns. The optimalist, on the other hand, accepts the fact that painful emotions are an inevitable part of being alive. He leaves room for sadness and pain. He knows that these feelings will also increase his overall experience.

"The optimalist knows that in an authentic life, you take the good with the bad".

On the contrary, the perfectionist is never satisfied, he constantly sets objectives and standards that are in all respects impossible to achieve, rejecting from the beginning any possibility of success. Whatever achievement, whatever thing it has, is never enough for its standards. He is signing the recipe for his unhappiness. He does nothing but rejecting the success of his life, because, despite the many goals achieved, he never perceives the feeling of success. He does not appreciate them and he does not enjoy them. He pays for the rejection of success, negative emotions and reality at a very high price. This rejection generates anxiety, because the possibility of disaster is always imminent. The refusal of pain leads to an intensification of the sensations that he attempts to repress, eventually causing even greater pain.

Exercise: **Learn from failures**, they are not so terrible. Take a quarter of an hour and write an event or situation where you didn't succeed. Describe what you did, the thoughts that crossed your mind, how you felt at that moment and how you feel now that you are writing it.

Has the passage of time changed your point of view on the event? What did you learn from that experience? Can you come up with other benefits as a result of the failure that made that event valuable?

Repeat this exercise two or three times on consecutive days within a week: you can write about the same failure or about another similar situation.

2.4 If only I could say what I think without fear ...

Anxiety brings with it the tension and fear of handling some arguments and conflicts. I know for sure that very often for fear of confrontation you happen to be excessively kind even with people who have a negative attitude towards you. It becomes crucial for you to learn rules that guide you in managing conflict and decrease the level of anxiety it brings. Peace at all costs is devastating. Perhaps you do not know that this "Conflictphobia" does nothing but increase the contrasts rather than reduce them. When, during an argument, we give in to other people's anger or allow someone to tyrannize or control us, we make a big mistake to ourselves, we feel very bad about it, our self-esteem goes down and our relationships suffer a lot, even if we don't realise it. We feel like victims of what happens to us when it is really our job to teach others how they should treat us, depending on how much we are willing to accept.

We always decide the border between what we tolerate and what we won't tolerate. Power is in our hands, it is our duty to make ourselves respected. But, to have personal power in a relationship of any kind, we must be willing to fight for ourselves and for what we think is right. This doesn't mean becoming mean or bad, there are rational and kind ways to be firm. Resoluteness is essential. This is why I will teach you some basic rules to keep in mind to promote your self-assertion and to express feelings in a firm but reasonable way, without being overwhelmed by negative emotions. We must learn to say no to situations and roles that falsify ourselves. This is how our liberation begins. With the discovery of the "no" we can avoid situations that do not fit us, away from all the rules that oppress us, and it is here that anxiety begins to disappear.

Advice for the management of conflictphobia. Here are 5 rules that will help you to establish yourself in a balanced way:

1.) Do not give in to the wrath of others just because it makes you uncomfortable.
2.) Do not allow other's opinions to influence your thinking. Your opinion must be the only one that matters, as far as possible. You should evaluate other's opinions in a non-submissive and critical manner.
3.) Say what you think and defend what you think is right.
4.) Keep self-control.
5.) Be kind, if possible, but above all, be resolute in your position.

"Remember that we teach others how to treat us".

If we give in to their outburst, we teach them that this is the way to control us. If we claim our ideas in a firm but gentle way, others will respect us more and will treat us accordingly. And if you have allowed someone to emotionally trample you for a long time, this someone will hardly accept your new attitude so there is just one thing to do: do not give up. Changes need repetition.

2.5 If only I could make a decision without feeling guilty ...

You are so full of guidelines, rules, things that should be done in a certain way, you listen to a myriad of people who tell you what to do that in the end you can no longer make a decision. It's a paradox: the more you search information, you try to be precise and meticulous, the more you increase your confusion. You live in the situation of the paradox of choice, that is, you believe that the more choices you have, the greater your freedom, and therefore your wellbeing. All of this is also deeply rooted in our society and in our life, so much that we consider it to be true. But let's pause for a moment:

"Is it exactly like that? Are we certain that being able to choose between many options guarantees our freedom?"

The answer is negative and I'll now explain to you why: when we have so many options, it becomes really difficult, not only to make the right choice, but to do it. Having so many alternatives produces, paradoxically, paralysis instead of protecting freedom. Paralysis is the direct consequence of having too many choices. There is no doubt that a little choice is better than not having any at all but this doesn't mean that having many choices is better than having one or two. This happens because we all need to have "limits": this allows us not only to have more control and awareness of what we are doing, and consequently, more satisfaction, but also to be able to overcome them.

But there is also another aspect to consider: you have learned very well to make choices that are more and more "external", more and more "right", more and more "conventional" but also more and more distant from your *being*, more and more *distant* from your inner centre. And here is the real problem. To satisfy everyone and never be criticized, you make choices that are gradually emptying you, depriving you of your vital energy with the result of feeling drained, emptied, and poorly satisfied.

It is pure madness to accept to be chronically anxious. Nobody wants life to be like this. You deserve to be happier and to find relief from the life that oppresses you. It is time to free yourself from external constraints and from those that you continually give yourself and it's time to be free and to act freely, this time according to your rules. From today onward you are the only one to dictate the rules of your life, which means regaining your natural disposition and so you will begin to distribute a quantity of energy that you didn't even realize you had, until now. This happens by the simple fact that your energy was stuck somewhere in your body, it was kept at bay by all the rules you had imposed upon yourself. Those problems you thought were insurmountable will slowly simplify, everything will be simplified, you will abandon the dimension of exertion and effort to embrace the magic of a simple, pure and beautiful life. An ideal life that you still struggle to believe it exists.

"Your life will heal"

The choices you will make will be your medicine and only then you can say you have achieved the true goal: to be yourself.

Tips

1) **Learn to lighten up**: not everything is a test, not everyone is waiting to see you be wrong so that they can criticize you. In effect, most of the time no one is really interested in what you do. Sometimes it can be fun to disappoint other's expectation by not making the classic "good impression". It has a liberating function and most of the time you realise that your weaknesses are more appreciated than your usual fresh face.

2) **Ask for forgiveness, not for permission**: stop asking permission for everything you want to start to do. People will never say "yes, go and try", people do not risk, it is much easier to warn "well ... I would rather wait ... you never know ... maybe you could risk...", but it is also true that you will find very few obstacles when you have already taken an action. So, for all the things that are important to you, where it makes no sense to wait, don't ask for permission. Just do it and you will adjust the direction along the way. At most if you hurt someone, you will ask for forgiveness.

... Don't forget that if you want to see, you must act ...

Chapter 3

Learn to act: 3 techniques to release anxiety

Before going on, let's make a small summary of the previous chapters. The good news that comes from recent studies is that anxiety is only an excess of energy that when appropriately channelled, it can lead you to achieve exceptional results. Excess energy that you still cannot manage and that you try hard to control but you realize that the more you try the more it escapes your control. It makes you uncomfortable because you always have the feeling it may explode at any moment for no apparent reason. We have also said that it is blocking you and very often you avoid doing things that you like because you think about what possible negative consequence could happen, you always assume the worst. You are an expert in anticipating the most unlikely events. You are full of NAT (Negative Automatic Thoughts) that is slowly immobilizing your desire to live.

What is the result of this vortex of thoughts? Your life energy is stuck somewhere, you've hidden it so well, that even you don't know where it is.

But I also know, and here comes the exiting part, that what you want the most in the world is to free yourself from this annoying mood and I can finally help you. I know that when you feel overwhelmed you need a certain solution that can quickly alleviate your anxiety and help you find peace and tranquillity. For several years I have realized that the great majority of my friends, clients and family members suffer from a very strong anxiety. Everywhere, I see people that are angry, deeply unhappy and in a hurry. They are so overloaded with obligations, duties and rules that they have lost their will to live. So, I asked myself: how would their lives change if they learned how to handle this cauldron of excess energy? I've seen people break free from anxiety by ceasing doing all those things that made them suffer, ceased pretending to be someone else and starting to respect their nature.

The 21 steps in 21 days program will help you to get rid of anxiety and finally live the life you deserve. But, be careful, this gift you are giving to your life is a tool, and like any tool that works, even if it's user-friendly, you must learn how to use it. To be ready to start the program that I will suggest to you in the last chapter, it is therefore necessary to start with simple actions that allow you to adjust and manage your reactions and emotions. In the previous chapter we talked about all those thoughts that cross your mind during the day, now we will talk about what happens at the body level and how to free yourself from anxiety through basic body practices.

The key points of this chapter are:
1) Relaxation techniques
2) Meditation
3) Self hypnosis

Please consider the reading of this part of the book as a training to get ready for the final race, which is 21 steps in 21 days.

"If you want something you've never had
You must be willing to do something you've never done."-Thomas
Jefferson

3.1 Diaphragmatic breathing

Usually, we think we need a form of treatment to free ourselves from anxiety. Instead, I propose to my clients to start with what we already have. Mother Nature has already given us everything, we just have to learn how to make the best use of our weapons. The main instrument we have is breathing.

Has anyone ever taught you to breathe? My question may seem absurd, but often nobody does it and so we do not benefit from all the advantages of truly effective breathing.

Breathing heals, it's free and we have it in unlimited quantity. Fantastic, right? But let's first see what the purpose of breathing is. The body is a perfect machine, it has its own intelligence and it does nothing randomly. Breathing is functional to take oxygen from the air to put it into the body and then blow out all the waste products such as carbon dioxide. Every cell in our body needs oxygen to work. Without oxygen there is no life. And the brain cells are particularly sensitive to oxygen. Did you know, if they are deprived of it, they will die to death after only four minutes?

It has been proven that very slight changes in the oxygen content in the brain can alter the way a person feels and behaves. Learning to breathe correctly is therefore fundamental from all points of view.

Let's move on to the basic exercise to understand how you breathe.

1. Sit down and get comfortable. Close your eyes. Put one hand on your chest and one on your stomach. Breathe and follow the rhythm of your breathing, without changing it. Listen to it.

   Do you breathe with your chest or your stomach? Or with both? Write down the answer below

   ....
   ....

Now I can tell you what the correct model of breathing is without influencing the exercise you have just completed. In technical jargon we are talking about "diaphragmatic respiration", that involves the lower part of the abdomen, releasing healthy hormones in the system including endorphins (natural analgesic substances that help to relieve muscular tensions and pains). The breathing that involves the diaphragm can slow down, through the reduction of blood pressure, the heartbeat that tends to be accelerated when we feel anxious, stressed or agitated.

2. To correct and / or train to breathe correctly, follow two simple steps:

 - Lie on your back and put a small book on your stomach;

 - When you inhale, make sure that the book rises, when you aspirate make it go down.

By moving the centre of our breathing to a lower part of your body, you will immediately realize that you are more relaxed and you have more self-control. Generally speaking, if you suffer from anxiety, you have an inverted breathing. Which means, to put it simply, that when you inhale the stomach deflates while when you exhale the stomach inflates. This breathing does nothing but worsen the situation so I invite you to spend 5-10 minutes a day on diaphragmatic breathing to make this knowledge permanent..

3.2 Focused meditation

There is a voice in our head that sometimes is unbearable. It begins to whisper each morning as soon as we open our eyes and it bothers us all day, even at night. It is a set of impulses, desires, opinions and thoughts that focus on the past and on the future, at the expense of our present. The same mechanism makes us open the fridge when we are not hungry, it makes us lose patience when we are aware that behaviour will be to our disadvantage or it drives us to monitor messages while we are engaged in a face to face conversation. Obviously, this inner voice is not something only negative, sometimes it's creative, generous and fun but if you can't handle it, and few of us know how to do it, it can turn out to be an evil puppeteer.

Then how to stop it?

The first and simple practice to learn is meditation, which is nothing but a brain workout. It is a proven technique useful to restrain the inner voice that distracts us from the tasks in which we are engaged, which stresses and alarms us.

Why is it so important to meditate?

It's simple, meditation reactivates the brain! It is no coincidence that it is used by managers, athletes and professionals to improve and achieve their goals, reduce dependency and avoid being overwhelmed by emotions.

It is considered the gateway to our essence. In fact, we are all in constant struggle, looking for a balance between who we really are and how we show ourselves. Meditation helps us to fill this gap to finally release our inner voice. How freeing! In addition, meditation training offers innumerable benefits, from improving health to greater concentration ability and finally reaching a feeling of calm, peace and harmony. But the biggest advantage is learning to "respond" rather than "react" to stimuli and events. Through meditation you will learn the art of being fully aware of whatever you are doing and accepting the present moment without having to express a judgment or an assessment. We are aware when we focus on the "here and now", when we allow ourselves to feel any emotion, regardless of whether we appreciate what we are experiencing or not. It means adopting a soft attitude towards oneself by renouncing the need to control ourselves and accepting the idea that there is something about us that we do not know yet.

Living with a soft attitude means starting to say to yourself:

"I am like this, I do not have to prove anything and I can be a passive spectator of myself".

This means living moments in which *I do not claim anything from myself, in which I like myself as I am, I do things as I can and because I want to do them.* This sounds exactly what you need, isn't it? If so, then try to experience meditation through this simple exercise.

Please follow all the steps without going on your own way, do not take initiatives that differ from the steps described in order not to risk compromising the outcome of the practice. Be precise, especially the first few times and repeat the exercise for five consecutive days.

Take 20 minutes just for yourself. Choose a precise moment of the day, in the morning when you have just woken up or before going to sleep is better. In fact, in these moments, your brain goes through the "theta phase", that is the mental state in which you mix imagination and reality (we'll explain it more thoroughly in one of the next paragraphs), so it will be much easier to relax and get in touch with your body.

Choose relaxing music, better if it is around 432 Hz. The human body is actually coded to receive music at 432 Hz because this is the vibration that can resonate with human cells. To find it, just go on YouTube and write "relaxing music 432 hz".

Find a comfortable position. I suggest you lie down on your back on the bed and put a pillow under the sheets.

Close your eyes. Relax the muscles of the face. Relax the forehead and unclench your jaw. It will work better if you're in the dark.

Place your hands on your abdomen and start breathing. This way you can feel the abdomen inflate and deflate.

Focus all the attention on your breath. Not to change it but to observe it as it is and continues to breathe with calm. My advice would be to breathe in for five seconds, holding your breath for five seconds then five seconds breathing out. When you become more experienced with this breathing, you can increase your time, perhaps using the sequence inhale-hold-exhale in 8-8-8 seconds. The aim of this exercise is to make your breathing longer and deeper.

Keeping your hands on your abdomen and while exhaling put them closer to your navel, then let them slide to the end of your abdomen

when you inhale. Feel the air that crosses you until it gets to your stomach and then slowly and calmly exhale. Focus on the feeling of your stomach that inflates when you inhale and deflates when you exhale.

Now concentrate on a memory or a positive image that gives you profound peace and then alternate this moment with others of complete mental emptiness. Try to completely clear your mind for a few seconds and then return to be nourished by the feelings of the positive memory.

Take note. Once finished, as soon as you feel ready, note the pleasant sensations you are feeling:

How's your breathing?

....
How's your heartbeat?

....
How are the muscles of the face?

....
 How do you feel within your body?

....

Remember once again to exercise every day with continuity and dedication. It's a moment where there is only you, where all the worries can wait, but above all, remember to always let yourself be guided by this question: "What's the most important thing for me, at the moment?" To have a break, relax, and calm down? Well, it's time to do it.

N.B. If during the exercise you get distracted, don't worry, it's completely normal at first but try to bring your attention back to the movements of your abdomen, returning to what you were imagining. If instead, you feel like crying do not hold back the tears, if other emotions like anger, disappointment or fear emerge, do not avoid them. If a part of the body reacts in a certain way, you can shift the attention to that part and imagine breathing inside it without trying to change its state. Meditation is not only a technique for stress reduction but it's a real form of liberation. The ultimate goal is to achieve emotional freedom! Are you ready to fly?

3.3 The self-hypnotic visualization

We have just learned how to breath and how to meditate through simple and specific exercises, now we will learn a technique you have probably already heard of, often in a negative way: self-hypnosis. Hypnosis is indeed a natural phenomenon and it has nothing to do with persuasion, much less with manipulation.

Self-hypnosis is necessary to soothe anxiety and achieve all our goals. It works because it relies on a natural energy source of our body that can calm our basal ganglia (that brain structure that becomes overactive when we get anxious). Self-hypnosis allows us to focus our concentration without the help of a hypnotist.

Have you ever been so absorbed by a good book or a good movie that two hours seemed like a few minutes? There it is. In these circumstances we focus so much that we enter a hypnotic state. Hypnosis is also used as a healing method which can slow down the brain waves of our brain and relax the body, thanks to the activation of the parasympathetic system which is responsible for the natural self-healing mechanisms of our body.

Now let's move on to the **self-hypnosis exercises**

Step 1: Sit down on a comfortable chair with your feet firmly resting on the floor and your hands on your lap.

Step 2: Choose a point on the wall located a little higher than the level of your eyes and fix it while slowly counting to 20. You will notice that, at some point, the eyelids will get heavy and then let the eyes close. If they do not close, close them slowly by counting to 20.

Step 3: Take a deep breath, as deep as possible and exhale very deeply. Repeat this deep breathing by slowly exhaling 3 times.

Step 4: Squeeze the muscles of the eyelids by squinting, then slowly relax. Then imagine that your relaxation spreads from the muscles of the eyelids down to those of the face, the chest and then to the rest of the body until it reaches the soles of the feet.

Step 5: Once relaxed, imagine yourself on top of an escalator and start to go down counting from 20 to 0.

Step 6: Enjoy a bit of tranquillity, then go back to the escalator and get on again. Count to 10. At 10 open your eyes and you will feel relaxed, awake and energetic.

To remember these steps more easily, think of the following words:

1) CONCENTRATION

2) RESPIRATION

3) RELAXATION

4) DOWN

5) UP

When you do this exercise the first few times, take some time. After practicing this technique a few times, I suggest you experiment it with a variation:

Add a visual image: choose a special shelter, a place where you feel good and you can imagine employing all your senses. It can be a real or imaginary place, it doesn't matter. E.g. after you get to the bottom of the escalator, imagine you're in your shelter. Continue to breath and relax, now your mind is ready to make you experience something new: to be as you want to be, not as you usually are but how you want to be, there is a big difference. Imagine, dream, exaggerate because the more you live this experience, the more it will become real.

3.4 Why should I adopt the techniques?

I didn't teach you these techniques just for fun. Relaxation, meditation and self-hypnosis are indispensable techniques for your state of mind, you must start considering them as real medicines. Anxiety blocked you, it's true, but it happened in the past and even if you wanted to improve the situation, it got out of your hand. Actually, on those occasions you didn't use right methods to free yourself from anxiety. But the past no longer exists, now the situation is changing, you are becoming more and more experienced in mastering your thoughts and your bodily reactions, but to master them completely you must constantly practice the techniques I have taught you. I really insist on perseverance, repetition is the mother of all abilities and every success needs continuous and constant improvements. You have been taught that if you are anxious you must learn to "live with it" saying the old same sentence:

But today you can tell all those who have demotivated you that it's possible to change, to live a life without anxiety, if we are willing to break the patterns. But let's go back to our techniques. Why is it so important to meditate, to breathe well and practice self-hypnosis?

For many reasons, but primarily because they are fast and immediately allow us to use the functioning mechanism of our brain.

You must know that our brain releases waves that, depending on the frequency, are divided into:
• **Delta:** characterized by a frequency ranging from 0.1 to 3.9 hertz, they are typical of the deep sleep phase.
• **Theta**: ranging from 4 to 7.9 hertz, they characterize the state of deep relaxation.
• **Alpha**: frequency ranging from 8 to 13.9 hertz, are typical of when we are awake and relaxed.
• **Beta**: ranging from 14 to 30 hertz, they are recorded when we are in a waking state, during intense mental activity or under stress.
• **Gamma**: from 30 to 42 hertz, they characterize the states of particular tension.

To overcome anxiety, the secret is to set up your brain chemistry on a relaxed and healthy level, that is on the alpha or theta brain waves. Being able to reach the alpha or theta state (this last one is typical of very deep meditation states and therefore requires a lot of exercise) will have many effects, including the improvement of:
- anxiety
-heartbeat rhythm
- blood pressure
- tension and muscular pains
- sex and libido
- hormone secretion
- the immune system

Isn't that reason enough?

The use of diaphragmatic breathing, meditation, and self-hypnosis is therefore essential to maintain the equilibrium of our body, our "homeostasis", which is indispensable for keeping us alive, let alone to feel good. These techniques are effective because they allow you to get access to emotions by acting through the body. Do you remember that body and mind are the same thing? We can therefore act on the body to alleviate tensions, worries and anxieties. It is no coincidence that we feel the emotions in the body and not in the head. When we start to breathe well, when our heart beats at a regular rhythm (to be precise we need to talk about "cardiac coherence", when the alternation of acceleration and deceleration of our rhythm is regular) our body is in equilibrium. If we look at our autonomic nervous system, we discover that it consists of two branches. The sympathetic system is active when we are under stress and overwhelmed by anxiety (it is not always negative, it saves us from dangers, the problem is that we activate it too often without real danger). The parasympathetic system, on the contrary, is responsible for activating the relaxation reaction, essential for healing and flourishing. Here, between these two branches there must be equilibrium (what we have called "cardiac coherence") and when it is lacking it's because we increasingly unbalance it with our thoughts, emotions and actions towards the stress system. It then breaks down and problems begin to arise, including anxiety, mood swings even causing real physical illnesses. I ask you to imagine your body is like a car: you cannot always keep your foot on the gas but you cannot always press the brake, in both cases you'll end up in causing damage.

"Your body is like a car, it works when the accelerator and brakes work in mutual harmony."

Remember: "95% OF PHYSICAL AND PSYCHOLOGICAL DISEASES ARE CAUSED BY STRESS AND 100% OF THE STRESS IS LINKED TO NEGATIVE CONVICTIONS -Dr. Lipton an evolutionary biologist.

What else is there to say?

Now it's time to change and to give everything you have. No excuse, no alibi. It makes no sense to wait. It makes no sense to delay. Tomorrow will never come. Now is the right time to wipe out everything you don't want to do, melt the blocks that bind you to the past and turn anxiety into creative energy. So practice, don't spare yourself, do whatever you feel like doing. Respect the commitment you have made with yourself.

Chapter 4

Anxiety without Sex or Sex without Anxiety?

In collaboration with Giuseppina Pollino

4.1 Feminine anxiety & Masculine anxiety

By this point in our reading you have become a little psychologist yourself, you have started to understand how you *works* and you know what triggers your friend anxiety. You know well that the anxiety you feel is linked to your personality, to your thoughts, to what you say constantly and to what you have been taught by the system in which you live. What we have not yet talked about is how anxiety also affects your sex life. It's very likely that you have thought many times that if something is not right when you are in bed, the fault is something physical or something is wrong with you or your partner, but remember that sexual difficulties are nothing but a bodily manifestation of a relational or individual problem. In other words, the body tells you something that you don't want to hear. Unfortunately, anxiety also permeates the intimate sphere with some subtle differences between men and women. There is a very funny book, which I invite you to read, titled "Men Are from Mars, Women Are from Venus" and explains very well how the same experiences, feelings and emotions are expressed differently, sometimes opposite, by man and woman. And now let's see how this difference between the two sexes also concerns anxiety.

Anxiety for women

The main characteristic of women with anxiety is their persistence in wanting to keep everything under control. They force themselves to follow fixed existential paths, they always do the same things in the same way and they have a very strong sense of duty. Their mind is full of rules, ideals and moralism. They tend to organise and plan everything. They give great importance to the opinions of others from which they are deeply influenced.

Let's move on to the identikit of anxiety women:

Control Women: deep-rooted inclination towards organization and planning. These are strict and performing women who live with the aim of being able to keep everything under control and excel in all areas. Living with the obsession of organising everything makes them easily predisposed to anxiety and panic. This constant attention to keep everything under control actually hides the most tender and sweet parts of this woman, as well as the most passionate and creative ones.

Maniacal Women: They are obsessed with order and cleaning, they keep their deepest impulses caged in a series of structures because they consider them to be dangerous. This is a desperate attempt to avoid listening to them because they are perceived like a threat to their balance.

Virile Women: They insist on proving to themselves and to other people that they are tough, strong and unshakable. They can do perfectly without men (or they believe so). Obviously, this willingness to be like a man at all costs, however, sacrifices their sweetness, their sensuality and their femininity because they are interpreted as forms of weakness. Here anxiety has lain claim to their feminine, sweet and most tender parts of their personality.

Dominant Woman: She shows her command, power, and security. Generally, she is an extremely dominant woman and also during sex she tends to exert this domination with an extreme and uninhibited Eros. It is a shame that anxiety, sometimes, goes knocking on her door reminding her that maybe she is not so confident.

Anxiety for men

And then we have male anxiety. Usually anxiety man offers an impeccable, super-efficient and perfect image of himself, or at least he thinks the world sees him that way. He's always right, he is never wrong and he trusts his opinions with conviction. He is sure of himself, he always knows what he wants, what he must and can do. He is very critical against those who think differently from him and is absolutely intolerant of others' mistakes. He hates anyone who breaks the rules and is always the one who leads the game. Let's see the identikit of the anxiety man.

Command Man: At work, at home, with friends, in the family, he always decides everything. But is he really a leader? Not really. Actually, he doesn't truly accept contradictions, for him there is only black and white. Fussy, meticulous and perfectionist. Very reliable. Very rigid in his choices, absolutist in judgments, he hates unpredictability. He shows the clear self-confidence that can only be the manifestation of the fear for the grey areas and insecurity

Automaton Man: perfectly in line with external models. He imitates and adapts himself in accordance to what is deemed the most acceptable. He is very careful to check any of his excesses, be it positive or negative. He adapts himself to its environment for fear of rejection. It tends to mask everything which is not compliant. The thing that he fears the most is to be alone, this would violently clash him with himself.

Fearful Man: Fearful, undecided, he always feels at fault. He suffers from terribly guilty feelings that prevent him from acting in all areas of his life and slow down his every decision. He believes that others expect great things from him and at the same time, he doesn't feel good enough nor does he wants to show himself to be weak. He doesn't accept his fragility and by doing so, only panic can make him show fragility.
In all these "types", anxiety breaks in as an energy that sweeps away with violence these two opposing forces, between the will to assert himself at all costs, and the unconscious desire to let go and give in.

4.2 Performance anxiety

At this point it is easy to understand how these personality characteristics, even if different, can jeopardise sexual life in a blink of an eye. Just a momentary thought such as "I wonder if I can please her" (in the case of men) or "I wonder if I can have an orgasm" (in the case of women) and the moment that, by definition, must to be lived in the most complete emotional freedom, is already ruined.

This happens because the focus becomes about the "performance" as the achievement of the objective and as confirmation of its validity. Some people develop real sexual disorders such as the decline in chronic sexual desire, the inability to achieve orgasm, premature ejaculation and dyspareunia. Even in these most extreme cases, however, it is always the discomfort in managing emotions, the lack of spontaneity, the excessive control that hinders a free and peaceful expression of sexuality. It is a complete contradiction: sex that serves to regenerate, to live according to our innermost nature, is once again experienced as a duty. It is a perverse dynamic but it's what naturally happens when we live a life based on inflexibility, rigor and perfectionism.

How can we not carry the same pattern in sex? Impossible! Fear of failure during sexual intercourse, fear of not achieving orgasm, the expectation of an idealized sexual performance and fear of rejection by the partner are the most frequent fears that penalise our sexuality. The most worrying thing is that, as time goes by, these behaviours solidify and take the form of a real "Performance Anxiety". But that's not all: once strengthened, it becomes a habit, a normality and to manage it we will begin to take defensive behaviours, trying once again to drive away the anxiety by sacrificing sexual pleasure. How? Through excessive observation and control over our emotions and reactions during the sexual act. We are facing the phenomenon that is commonly called "Spectator Effect" that is self-observation while making love, as if we were a judge of ourselves. Do you know what the result is? The loss of our spontaneity, of our instincts, the negation of our personality, and of pleasure. In a word: self-destruction.
But it's not finished here. Another common defensive behaviour that unconsciously and erroneously is taken to appease anxiety is to completely deprive ourselves of erotic feelings. We say that "we are not interested, that there will be time, in the future, to think about this, which is not important now, it's not for now, it's not needed". We begin to show indifference to those sensual and exciting sensations that we should live normally during these moments of intimacy. Above all, we avoid people who we find more attractive and the fear that hides behind it is that of failure. We feel like we are being tested, we think we are not perfect to overcome the test that will sanction the judgment we will have of ourselves.

As I said, it is the lack of spontaneity, the excessive control, the inflexibility to cause the most frequent intimate problems with one's partner. With the arising of these sexual difficulties, if we do not proceed through the use of daily exercises (which we will explain later), or sex therapy for the more persistent cases, we will also risk to affect the sphere of desire. The arising of a terrible anticipatory anxiety will actually cause the total avoidance of the sexual relationship in a short time and a feeling of resignation, which is linked to the forever abandonment of the extraordinary sensation of "sexual pleasure", will follow. We will begin to tell us that the situation will not be solved, that it will always be worse and that nothing will work for us. Fortunately, we know and the studies confirm it, that this condition of "resignation" is dynamic and it can be changed; it is a phase and as such, it is enough to overcome it and move on to a new and more stimulating one.

How?

You need two ingredients:

1. **Active and constant participation in the process**. Follow the anxiety management exercises suggested with dedication and continuity;
2. **Strong motivation to be a sexually satisfied person.**

Do you think you have it?

If you already think you have these two motivational ingredients, then it's already 50% of the work done. But before going on to the practical phase, let's recap: now you know this enemy (or maybe friend) called "Anxiety", you know what it represents, what its message is, you have accepted its presence, you learned to manage it thanks to the questions have asked yourself, to the techniques and the exercises proposed in this book. It has become a part of you, your energy!

Now I want to reveal another secret:

Sexuality is also energy and as such, it is part of everyday life. Sex represents the relationship with the other and sometimes you have transferred your fears and insecurities under the sheets. You did not notice it but I assure you it happened. But now it's time to put in place everything you've just learned. But to make sure you have given yourself a complete list of tools to overcome anxiety in all its facets, I suggest the following program of specific exercises for the management of anxiety in sexuality.

These are exercises to be carried out over a minimum of three weeks. I don't want to be demanding but I want to avoid you being hasty and cutting corners. Remember that rushing is the enemy of sex. You must recognize that sex has its natural flow and wants to be left alone. It wants to express itself in total harmony and relaxation. It badly coexists with the

objectives and with the imposed obligations. So, don't mind the time, just slow down consciously. Trust me, if you're not in a hurry, it works. For this reason, you must follow the suggestions and be careful not to follow your hurried intuition. Proceed through the various stages only when you feel ready. Are you wondering what it means to be ready? I'll answer you right away: when you feel you are driven only by desire, a pure desire, untied by everything else. I'm talking about that desire that you cannot stop even when it is really forbidden. There are no objectives nor performances to achieve, delete these words from your vocabulary during these three weeks.
You can perform these exercises either individually or in pairs.

What are these exercises for?

1. Deconditioning yourself: unblock mental associations that you link to sex.
2. Approach yourself in a gradual and progressive way to the enjoyment of those feelings of tenderness and eroticism that have been put aside for too long.

It's fundamental that you proceed without haste but also without interruptions

4.3 Goodbye performance anxiety: the program in 3 weeks

1st week

1- Create a reassuring environment and a right atmosphere.

You can also help yourself with the use of candles, music at very low volume, sheets and pillows that you like or a pretty underwear.
Remove all forms of distraction, books, computers, television or telephone. If you are feeling particularly tense, help yourself with a glass of wine.
This preparation phase is really important: feeling comfortable and at ease

with your own body and your environment will have a reassuring and relaxing effect.

2- Take a step-by-step interaction with your partner.
Make sure to proceed gradually and very slowly. There is no goal to be reached, you have all the time, you do not have to decide anything, think as if your brain was detached and can only be guided by the indications of this exercise.

3- Undress, look at your partner and only then caress the body of each other in turn, starting from the head, neck and down to the feet.
No part of the body should be neglected. You can linger more on some parts. The caresses and kisses must concern the whole body, with the exception of the genitals, and can be deep and lasting.

4- If you prefer, you can give yourself a time (preferably 10/15 minutes each) and enjoy it until the last second.
It is important that both of you enjoy the same quality time. I recommend caressing each other alternately so that everyone can focus on their own sensations. You decide together who, out of the two partners, start touching the other and then abandon yourself to the feeling of that moment You must learn to live the images, the looks, the words, the sighs, the feeling of warmth, the skin and the curves and understand what they evoke in you. Imagine yourselves as innocent and curious, like you have never experienced these sensations before.

5- Admire and let yourself be admired

Try to stay deeply focused and every time you get distracted, turn your focus to what you are doing at that moment. Even if you feel excited and you would like to go further, you do not have to give in; it's still too early, you still have to learn something about yourself. So, accept your excitement but don't follow it and return to the exercise.

6- Repeat the exercise during the first week for a minimum of two times.

Before starting, talk about this program with your partner, making clear that this will not be a massage aimed at the sexual act but only to the mutual knowledge of your bodies and your pleasure. Agree with him / her when you can take some time out for yourself and do not worry if you initially feel that the exercise is somewhat clumsy. It is also perfectly possible that you feel uncomfortable, but do not worry because you are both trying it for the first time and the only way to overcome it is to use humour: have a good laugh and take it as a game with specific rules.

7- Report of the first week. At the beginning of the second week, together make a brief analysis of how you feel about the "sex" issue. The mere fact of having performed these exercises 2/3 times should have already reduced the level of anxiety linked to the relationship. By simply playing and approaching sex without being forced to have complete intercourse has created new convictions linked to sex that are much more harmonious and reassuring. Moreover, you have learned new things about yourself and your partner.

So, based on your feelings, you have two alternatives for the second week:

- repeat the exercises of the past week;

- move on to the second phase and onto the new task.

The choice depends on the degree of serenity and curiosity: simply continue if you feel ready for the new step and have fun at the idea. On the contrary, if you want to continue only because you are driven by the rush to finish the program or you still feel you want to consolidate the feelings of last week there's no problem, give yourself another week for yourself and repeat the exercises.

2nd week

When you feel that physical contact is no longer associated with feelings of anxiety, we arrive at the second phase which also includes the genitals. Now you can remove the underwear and even caress the genitals like any other part of the body. You can give yourself time, at least 10 minutes each and you can share your fantasies with the partner. Even here there may be erections or lubrications and the same principle applies: accept them and fully feel them and then return to the exercise. At this point of the program you and your partner will have exponentially decreased performance anxiety as the goal of this exercise is not to feel excited or conclude sex but to experience all the sensations that come spontaneously without following or forcing them. Also for this second week, I suggest you repeat the exercises at least twice. I advise you not to do this more than four times because we must re-establish a progressive rhythm and therefore it isn't necessary to exaggerate.

3rd week

At the beginning of the third week, you can add a novelty to the sensory focus of the previous week. While you are busy touching, caressing, kissing and admiring yourself, the one who is receiving the "massage" can direct the partner's hand, as if it were a guide of your body and of your own pleasure. By now, you are aware of your erogenous points and your own fantasies and so you can share with your partner the details that are difficult to express in words. An exchange of information in positive but not distracting terms can be useful, only if it's accepted by both and lived without judgment . I remind you that even at this stage it is required that the whole procedure is carried out in a context of a relaxed and non-demanding atmosphere in which penetration is excluded. Take full advantage of the delicate and magical moments that you are experiencing, consider them as exciting tools that you can use even when the anxiety will be gone. Just play and increase the desire of the partner and yours.

Conclusions

We know that sensory focusing works. It helps to overcome possible sexual problems such as erectile dysfunction, vaginism, difficulty in achieving orgasm but it is also an excellent remedy for male and female performance anxiety. When we are anxious, the flow of waiting, of desire, of fantasy is completely blocked. Before proceeding with the sexual intercourse, we must inevitably remove every concern and every goal from the sexual field. Approaching pleasure and experiencing it in its intermediate forms helps to effectively re-familiarise with sex. In these moments, putting aside the idea of perfectionism, of achievements and of performance is already reassuring us that we can do it. It recognises our fear and supports it. Not having to do anything or achieve something reassures us and allows us to experiment, and when we experiment we are curious and free and in this situation, everything will be for the best. Sensory focusing, through a gradual exposure to sexuality, makes us revive progressively all the pleasures that have been affected by anxiety. Not only that: it stimulates our curiosity and the discovery of erogenous zones, desires, forms of contact that are sexually exciting but that we didn't know yet. And finally, it promotes communication between partners on sexual issues that are generally considered taboo. and this new competence is the one that guarantees the sexual success of the couple. Without transparent communication, we could never fully live a rich, free and fulfilling sexual life. At the end of the three weeks, you will have a clearer idea of what was hindering your intimate life. And you will find yourself facing one of these three scenarios:

1) You will be rediscovered and all the anxieties will have vanished;

2) You will have understood how you feel about your partner: are you getting distant from each other?

3) You will have noticed an improvement and you will have realised that the sexual difficulties are not insurmountable and maybe you still want to fix the relationship and you will be able to turn to a specialist.

The lesson to learn is always the same:

*"There is no right or wrong way in life and even more in sex, there is only
a body that responds to our inner life, a body that doesn't lie, a body to
listen, that always reveals the truth about who we are and our deeper
desires".*

* Dr. Giuseppina Pollino, Psychologist and Sexologist, specialized in
performance anxiety and panic attacks. She carries out individual and
couple sexual counselling. She receives clients in her studio in Milazzo
and in Rome.

Chapter 5

Anxiety Lifestyle

5.1 Regenerative sleep

In this part we talk about LIFESTYLE and how to establish a **healthy way** of life. To begin with, we will focus our attention on SLEEP, or rather, on BAD SLEEP, one of the many possible consequences of being overwhelmed by anxiety. I refer to sleep disorders. The difficulty in unwinding also affects the moments of rest, making our nights "dynamic". Good quality of our sleep is essential to live well since it influences, in a directly proportional way, the quality of our day. If we sleep badly, in fact, our day will be negative; if instead we have a restful sleep, in the morning we will be energetic, alive and productive. The prognosis is certain: by knowing how well you slept, you will know how your day will be.
The more we have quality sleep, the greater the chances that our day will be peaceful, just like one night spent obsessing and worrying is enough to ruin the whole week. Even if we don't notice the deleterious effects of the sleepless nights immediately, you can be rest assured that in the medium and long term they will be felt. It's still the same old tale: the body whispers that something is wrong and initially does it subtly with some slight symptom, but if we continue to neglect its messages, there is nothing left it can do but start screaming.
I don't wish to sound melodramatic, I just want to make you understand how good sleep is the basis for living well. I still haven't met anyone with a poor quality of sleep who has a wonderful life: I really don't think they exist. The goal of this chapter is to set a healthy lifestyle so that anxiety doesn't find fertile ground to come out. Let's start with techniques that will allow you to improve the quality of sleep time with immediate effects on the quality of your day.

The three most frequent scenarios for those who cannot sleep well are:

- Not being able to get to sleep;

- Wake up too early in the morning and still feel tired;

- Continual nocturnal awakenings.

The risk lies in falling into a real "vicious cycle of bad sleep". After a few sleepless nights - a normal situation that can happen to everyone - we begin to think that it will happen again, we worry and we get anxious, with the only result of not sleeping or sleeping badly the next night. It is the magic of self-fulfilling prophecy: constantly thinking that a certain thing will happen creates the necessary conditions to make it happen for real.

Since it is your mental mechanisms that feed this cycle, it's time to change them, isn't it? Or do you want to continue spending nights at the mercy of negative thoughts? But if anxiety and stress feed bad sleep, the opposite is also true. This means that the lack of sleep or bad sleep increases the symptoms of anxiety. It isn't excluded, however, that a small percentage of anxious or stressed people do not show problems in the quality of sleep. The problem arises once again when the fear of not being able to fall asleep takes over, a feeling of not knowing what to do anymore. And here's again how anxiety can turn something instinctive and natural like sleeping in a complex and difficult mechanism. But now let's stop discussing the issue and start with a series of practical tips that, once internalized, will let you regain the pleasure of sleeping. Life changes when you sleep well.

The 4 strategies to sleep well

First thing to know: human minds are very sensitive to associations. I am sure that you, like anyone else, have a favourite place where to lay and relax. Thus, identify your favourite place, remove the elements that destabilize your sleep (lights, noises, and stressing factors) and create positive associations.

Let's move on to the strategy.

1st step: Check that the associations that get activated when you go to sleep facilitate your sleep.

If you suffer from insomnia, you have the habit of adopting behaviours that keep you awake, like playing with your smartphone or thinking about the list of the things to do the day after. Nothing could be more wrong. In doing so, you associate actions which require complicated processing and a vigilant mind, to the place where, by definition, one "must" sleep.

2nd step: Stop this association. Always keep in mind that there are only three things to do when you're in bed:
1. Sleep;
2. Making love;
3. Meditation exercises (as they help the mind to slow down by preparing for sleep).

3rd step: Develop a strong association between bedroom and sleep.
1. Use the bedroom only for sleeping. It is forbidden to read, stay at the PC or watch TV in bed;
2. Go to bed only when you are sleepy and if you cannot fall asleep, get up and go to another dimly lit room. Don't stay awake in the bed for too long, otherwise a strong association between staying in bed and staying awake will develop in your mind. It is harmful.

4th step: Train your brain to feel sleepy and awake at regular times.
1. Set a fixed time for going to bed and for waking up, for example at 10

pm in the evening and at 8.00 in the morning. The hardest thing, but also the most important, which hardly anyone does, is to stick to this schedule even on weekends, no matter how long you slept the day before. The brain needs repetitiveness to make a good habit permanent (it is still too early to transgress the program, when your sleep will be settled, you can change your schedule on the weekend).

Practical advice

What NOT to do:

1. Do not turn on the light if you plan on getting up at night to go to the bathroom. It would stimulate you too much.

2. Never take naps even if you need them. They reduce the unity of sleep.

3. Never go to sleep overstimulated or overexcited. TV, newspapers, Facebook are poison for your sleep. Stop using them at least two hours before going to sleep. Avoid discussions with the partner as well as studying or working after dinner. Postpone these activities to when you are full of your energy (usually in the morning).

4. Never sleep with the phone turned on. Turn off the phone when you sleep. The activities carried out on the cell phone in the night only prevents you from truly unwinding, which is needed for a good sleep. This is because the blue light emitted from the cell phone that flashes directly in the eyes inhibits the production of the sleep hormone, melatonin, upsetting your rest. Disconnecting yourself allows the mind to process and absorb all the adrenaline released as a reaction to the exciting images of the day, to slow down until it reaches a quieter course that will synchronize with the natural drive to sleep.

5. Do not drink after dinner. It would be ideal to drink the last glass of water 45 minutes before dinner. I know it can be difficult considering that most people satisfy their daily water needs during dinner, but in any case, try to do your best or, at the very least, don't drink after dinner.

6. Avoid alcohol. Although it might seem like alcohol helps you to fall asleep, since it initially causes a rapid rise in blood sugar which makes it easier to fall asleep. However, soon after it may cause you night awakenings that are difficult to manage.

7. Completely avoid the use of caffeine and tea. If you really can't do without it, start to gradually reduce them: after 3:30 pm it is better not to take them at all.

8. Avoid going to bed when stuffed. The feeling of heaviness interferes with sleep.

What TO DO

Create an environment that is favourable to sleep. Your room should be:

1. DARK: I advise you to get blackout curtains.

2. SILENT: reduce exposure to noises, if it's not possible, use earplugs, better if foamed and cylindrical.

3. FRESH: 18 ° C is the ideal temperature. The bed must be warm but the air in the room should be cool. When the air is too hot we tend to wake up.

4. COMFORTABLE: use a mattress and a comfortable pillow. If you wake up with muscle pain, perhaps your bed is not suitable for you. Do not procrastinate. Change it. The clock must not be clearly visible,

it is even better if there isn't one in the room.

SLEEPY TIME: create rituals that are associated with sleep.

Some examples:

1. Prepare an herbal infusion;

2. take a hot bath with Epsom or magnesium salts, especially if you feel tired in the evening;

3. use essential oils and floral essences, especially lavender ones to perfume the environment;

4. use a lavender mask to sleep;

5. do some progressive muscle relaxation exercise before going to bed, such as stretching or yoga;

6. choose a simple meditation technique that helps the mind slow down. 21 deep breaths can suffice.

Go to sleep before midnight. Remember: every hour before midnight is worth twice as hours of rest. The ideal would be to go to bed at 10pm and wake up at 6.00am. As usual my advice is to do your best, you do not have to be a robot, try to adapt any advice that I give you to your situation. If you go to sleep every day at 2.00 and you wake up at 10.00, then start by anticipating your sleep pattern and adjusting your body clock by an hour to gradually get to your ideal time.

Free your mind before going to sleep. If you really cannot avoid thinking about what you should do tomorrow, follow these three tips:

1) Prepare yourself for the following day and write down, as notes, all you need to do, prioritising them. Remove or postpone those that you would not be able to do anyway.

2) Reduce worries. Dedicate a specific moment of the day to reflection, to the organisation of that thought that worries you so that it does not erupt during your sleep. This moment must become a sort of ritual, for example, every day at 19.15 you decide to think about this specific situation so that it cannot interfere with your sleep.

3) If you are following a project where you need insights or ideas, it may be helpful to have a pen and paper near the bed to write down the ideas that may come to your mind while you are relaxing. Often it is precisely in this moment that the best intuitions emerge.
And if these techniques don't work, follow this exercise:

Leave the day behind

We know that for many people, the moment they go to sleep coincides with the first time they really manage to relax since they got up and, considering that, we unfortunately don't always have the opportunity to record all the events of the day and absorb them. We may happen to have a roller coaster of troublesome thoughts that prevents us from unwinding. An excellent solution is to return to each event in reverse order so that it's possible to identify them one by one and process all the emotions they gave you. I'll explain how to do it in three simple steps:

1. Mentally visualise what you were doing just before going to bed, continue to visualise all the previous actions until you go back to all the events of the day, one at a time, until you get to the moment you woke up in the morning.

2. For each event you will have a compressed memory but once they are organised in sequence, you will remember the key emotions of the day you have just lived.

3. Now that you have reorganised everything and the chaos has become clarity, you are ready to sleep.

5.2 Food and mind supplements

If the body changes, the mind changes ...
If the mind changes, the body changes ...

Body and mind are the same thing and that's why, when we change the emotions we live, we feel much better physically, less bloated and more energetic. This is also the reason why that if we change our eating habits we will have great improvements also in mood and anxiety. Some foods calm anxiety and others do exactly the opposite.

Some types of food can have a negative effect on your mental health and physical condition and you don't know it.

What to avoid:

1) sugars
2) refined carbohydrates,
3) alcoholic beverages

1. Do not consume any form of added sugars, neither natural nor artificial. No table sugar, maple juice, honey, agave juice, stevia, aspartame, xylitol, saccharin, sucralose, acesulfame, dextrose, maltodextrin, etc. Read carefully the food labels because these substances are added into many foods in which you do not suspect they are present.

2. Do not consume refined carbohydrates. Eat whole grains but avoid wheat (bread, pasta, flour) rye, kamut, emmer wheat and barley. On the contrary, rice, corn, buckwheat, millet, quinoa, amaranth and oat are all very good.

3. Do not consume alcohol. Eliminate alcohol from your everyday diet, it's obvious that at the weekend or during an evening with friends it is permitted, at least to ease up and loosen up.

What to eat:

Eat unprocessed and whole foods. Returning to a healthy diet means taking back nature. Consume foods with few ingredients, ingredients with a pronounceable name, or even better, without artificial ingredients because they will be natural and not processed.

Carbohydrates: Studies have shown that "true" whole grains cereals are very good for people who suffer from anxiety because they are rich in magnesium, they contain tryptophan that turns into serotonin, they give energy and at the same time reduce the sense of hunger.

Protein: Try to prefer fish to meat. Eat red meat in moderation. Eggs, legumes, yogurt, ricotta and goats milk products are particularly known for the high content of tryptophan.

Vegetables: make sure that vegetables are your main dish and that they never leave your table. Better if raw or steamed.

Fruit: all fruits are good, but the best are the red fruits. Red fruits are a class of food with enormous therapeutic value. Strawberries, cherries and berries (blackberries, raspberries, blueberries, redcurrants and blackcurrants) are considered "super foods" because they are rich in vitamins and phytonutrients (plant nutrients), with a high percentage of antioxidants, a great help to relieve stress. Many experts believe that peaches also fall into this category because they contain nutrients that seem to have a calming effect.

Oilseeds: Almonds, hazelnuts, nuts and seeds should always be in our diet. They are excellent for nourishing our mind. Almonds are an undervalued food. They contain zinc, a fundamental nutrient to maintain a balanced state of mind, together with iron and the so-called healthy fats. Healthy fats play an important role in a diet, while iron deficiency is responsible for brain fatigue, which leads to anxiety and lack of energy. Personally, I love cocoa beans and, in general, raw cocoa, which can be considered an excellent supplement to a healthy diet because of their characteristics. They act as natural performance enhancer and stimulants of the nervous system but they also have antidepressant and antioxidant properties. Especially pure dark chocolate, without milk or added sugar, is an excellent food for those who suffer from anxiety or stress. Chocolate is not only a natural antidepressant but also reduces cortisol, the hormone responsible for stress that causes anxiety symptoms. Maca root, also known as "Peruvian ginseng" (even though it does not belong to the ginseng family) cannot fall short in your storeroom because it is used as a folk remedy to increase energy and sexual functions. It is thought that this root contains more phytonutrients of any other kind of fruit or vegetables, such as magnesium and iron, two substances important for controlling anxiety

Fats and oils: the brain is made of 60% fat, so it is important to reintegrate the "good" ones with food. The main source is fish, rich in Omega 3 that help the membranes to remain healthy and improve mental alertness. Olive oil, butter (and ghee), coconut oil and avocado are also rich in good fats. Never underestimate how fat is fundamental to our mind. Our brain represents only 2% of the total weight of our body, but it is always "hungry" for energy and as such it needs good fats.

Water: the brain needs hydration. Many studies have shown that dehydration is a problem that affects at least 25% of people suffering from chronic stress and is one of the triggers of anxiety. So, try to respect your needs with this simple formula: for every 30 kg of weight you weigh, drink 1 litre of water a day.

When food is not enough, supplements come into play. How to choose the right ones.

Here below I will explain which supplements are useful for managing anxiety and why they work. They are guidelines to understand what you need, but always ask for advice from your doctor or get advice directly from the pharmacy on which products to choose before taking them.

- **Theanine**. L-Theanine is present in nature in the leaves of green tea (Camellia sinesis L.). Some studies in the literature have shown an increase in the production of alpha-cerebral waves after the intake of L-Theanine. Alpha-brain waves characterize a relaxed state of wakefulness and are responsible for focusing the attention during brain activity and thus, they support concentration and hinder the presence of interference information. There are many biological properties attributed to theanine but we only need to focus on its relaxing and anxiolytic effects to lower anxiety levels, improve sleep quality and relaxation.

- **Valeriana extract.** It owes its name to the Latin "valere" that means "stay healthy". Valeriana (Valeriana officinalis L.) is traditionally used to facilitate relaxation, thanks to its precious soothing properties that make it a natural remedy, especially in cases of anxiety and stress. It is a good remedy even in the evening, thanks to its effect that promotes a restful sleep.

-**Rhodiola**. Also known as Golden Root or Arctic Root. The Rhodiola Rosea L. has been used in traditional Eurasian medicine for over three hundred years for its versatility as an herbal tonic. The root of Rhodiola acts as a tonic-adaptogen counteracting physical and mental fatigue, acting on both the physical and mental levels. Rhodiola Rosea, in fact, has an energizing and invigorating effect, especially in preparing the body to bear tiredness by raising the tolerance limit. From the mental point of view, it is an excellent anti-stress, which helps to recover from prolonged exhaustion linked to particularly "strenuous" periods of life. In this respect, it especially acts at the level of the sympathetic system, against anxiety and depression, increasing (up to 30%) the levels of serotonin in the blood, which is responsible for the feeling of wellbeing, and opposing the negative effects of cortisol, which is produced by the adrenals in case of high stress. It also acts on the intellectual level, improving memory and concentration, thanks to the action on dopamine and norepinephrine. In addition it reduces mental fatigue and raises our threshold of attention. Rhodiola Rosea enhances brain function in general, giving more lucidity and making people more disposed to act, as well as being a good remedy for insomnia. To be clear, it is enough to know that the Rhodiola acts in three ways: it reduces stress, raises the mood and improves the quality of sleep.

5-HTP (5-hydroxytryptophan). Tryptophan is the precursor of serotonin, the so-called "good-mood hormone". 5-HTP is extracted from the seeds of Griffonia Simplicifolia, an African tropical plant. Serotonin is one of the main neurotransmitters in the nervous system, which transmits messages between nerve cells and is involved in the regulation of mood, hunger and sleep. In particular, low levels of serotonin are associated with various forms of mood alteration, excessive apprehension, difficult emotional management and in some cases, headaches. Moreover, serotonin, as a precursor of melatonin, intervenes in the quality of sleep. In summary, Griffonia extract improves mood, helps to sleep and decreases appetite.

-Vitamins B. Group B vitamins reduce tiredness and fatigue, help in the normal functioning of the nervous system and normal psychological function. Excellent for improving mental performance.

- Magnesium. Magnesium contributes to the normal functioning of the nervous system and of the psychological and muscular function, since it has a physiological myorelaxant and relaxing effect. It also counteracts tiredness and fatigue and contributes to normal energy metabolism, helping to turn the nutrients contained in food into energy.

- **Vitamin D**. You should be exposed to sunlight at least 15 minutes a day without sunglasses. Exposure to the sun increases the levels of vitamin D but, contrary to what we have always been told, you should expose to sunlight without the use of sunscreen since, these block the UVB rays that trigger the production of vitamin D in the epidermis. Vitamin D is the most powerful natural antidepressant. A study published on FASEB Journal, for example, has shown that vitamin D acts on the TPH2 gene that transforms tryptophan into serotonin and, as you probably already know, serotonin is the so-called "well-being hormone". In fact, this important hormone regulates intestinal transit, sleep, appetite, mood and body weight. Low levels of serotonin are associated with depression and anxiety. It is easy to understand how much sun exposure is essential for our well-being, besides the fact that we are all good looking if we are a little more tanned.

5.3 Sport that frees anxiety

Physical activity is one of the best ways to get rid of toxins that stress accumulates in the body. Our muscles need to be exercised every day and, if this does not happen, there is a progressive loss of strength, endurance and agility, the muscles weaken and the body begins to accumulate energy (or calories) in the form of fat. It is now scientifically proven that physical activity promotes sleep and decreases the symptoms of anxiety.

But what kind of physical activity are we talking about?

We know that doing little physical activity is bad for health but too much physical activity hurts. How to regulate it then? An excellent system is to rely on heartbeat. It is very useful, in this regard, to buy a heart rate monitor, a small instrument consisting of a band to be applied to the chest and a clock which can monitor the number of beats per minute. At this point it is necessary to determine the ideal cardiac frequency in order to practice physical activities. If you have the opportunity to go to a qualified sports centre, they will certainly have the equipment to perform the measurement directly during the execution of the exercise. This method is certainly the best, because it allows maximum customisation. However, there is a do-it-yourself method and it's still valid to calculate it, through a simple mathematical formula which is the following:

180 – age +/ - 5 – 10

Let's take for example a person of 45.

180 – 45= 135

To this result we will remove:

- 10 if the person is obese or takes drugs;
- 5 if the person is inactive, has allergies or more than two colds a year;
- 0 if the person has been exercising for less than two years without problems.

We will add +5 if you have trained for more than two years. The value obtained represents the maximum reachable. Our heart rate during physical activity will have to fluctuate between that value and 10 beats less.

So, in the specific case of the 45-year-old woman, who we assume to have been physically active for less than 2 years without any problems, 135 is the maximum reachable value to which we have yet to remove 10:
135-10= 125

Ultimately, in the case reported, the heart rate during the activity will have to oscillate between 135 and 125, neither above nor below these values.

This type of sports program is aimed at not stressing the body too much and it will be organized as follows:
• for the first few months, you should practice aerobic activity at the ideal heart rate for only 30 minutes a day, every day;
• if you just cannot take some time for yourself every day, alternatively I recommend a minimum of 40 minutes, 3 times a week of sport activity;

• excellent examples of sports are running, aerobic gymnastics, swimming, dance, cycling, yoga, uphill walking and Nordic walking. Choosing the sport which you enjoy is always the best solution.
• Only after having developed sufficient aerobic capacity (after a month or so) you can add anaerobic activities once a week (for example weights, squats, lunges or isometric exercises, shadowed by a trainer).

As you may have guessed, what I propose is a moderate but continuous and progressive physical activity over the time. Now I'll explain why it works.

Moderate cardiovascular exercise reduces the activation of the sympathetic system (stress system) and modulates the release of cortisone (stress hormone). Therefore, at the beginning, since the level of accumulated stress or adrenal exhaustion is generally very high, a very light physical activity such as walking or a jog for 30 minutes is advisable. Also, make sure to try to keep constant attention on your body. Let me explain further. If you feel excessively tired after exercise, have backaches or other pains, it is very likely that there is adrenal insufficiency, caused by the inability of the adrenal glands to produce sufficient amounts of cortisol, an essential hormone for the organism. Your body is telling you that it would be better to reduce the intensity or duration of the exercise. Evaluate your body's reactions every day. I advise you to keep a diary or download one of the many apps to write down all the reactions of your body and to be able to figure out for yourself if you need to speed up or slow down the activity. If it is true that practicing physical activity at this intensity is usually good for the mind and the body, it is equally true that only you can determine what works best for you. The monitoring of your well-being is up to you, I can only give you advice. One last thing: since the sunlight has beneficial effects for both the immune system and the endocrine system, it is better to train during the day and in the open air, obviously if time and commitments allows it.

What else is there to say? I think that this is more than enough to begin with.

All that remains is to start with the program I've just suggested.

5.4 Yoga: the best antidote for anxiety

in collaboration with Alice Giusti *

Yoga was born in India thousands of years ago. The ancient practitioners discovered something exciting, that is, by awakening and moving the energy in the body, it was possible to reach such a condition of well-being and fulfilment in having full awareness of oneself. The tendency of man, today more than ever, is that of separating the body from the mind and it is this separation that causes stress, anxiety and suffering. Yoga fits into this picture and, through some focused and constant practices, helps us to rediscover our true nature, which has to do with the completeness and the union of body, mind and soul. It is not by chance that the word "Yoga" derives from the Sanskrit root "Yug" which means "to unite, to bind together." Yoga fundamentally allows the union of body and mind through a medium that we all have and it's unlimited: "breath". What we often forget is that the breath changes continuously according to the emotional state. Thus, we move from the suffocated breathing of fear, to the wheezing of anxiety and stress, to the long and deeply relaxed breathing of those in love.

Every movement of the body, every mental state is related to breathing and the main muscle is the diaphragm. Its uniqueness is immediately understandable if you think that, whilst being an involuntary muscle (like the heart), it is possible to control it. For those suffering from anxiety, this control is essential. Anxiety, stress, fear lead us to breathe badly, not allowing our body and mind to become one. The practice of Yoga, instead, teaches us to know our breath and to guide it, so that it's us who keep our emotions under control and it's not our emotions to control us, and all this is essential if you want to free yourself from anxiety.
We often look at ourselves in the mirror, we check the wrinkles that increase on the face or if our hair is well done, if we have put on some

extra weight on our waist, but we forget to observe how we are at a deeper level, who we really are, what scares us and why.

Those who practice Yoga learn over the time to look inside themselves, they become a spectator of their mind, their thoughts, their fears and their anxieties. As a spectator it is easier to understand, to impartially interpret and it is even easier to find a solution. During the practice we are alone with ourselves, we observe our thoughts and sensations, we listen to our body, we guide our breathing. And it's exactly the guidance of the breath that makes us take the reins of our emotions and allows us to overcome that state of anxiety that never makes us enjoy the present moment.

Those who are anxious tend to live in the past but especially in the future, they continually experience the stress of what has been and the anxiety of what will be. Yoga brings us to the present moment which is the only place where life exists. Life is now. Now is the time to understand what happens to our body and mind after having learned to master how to breathe, moving from an unconscious to a conscious and voluntary action.

Here is where the Autonomous Nervous System comes into play, the set of cells and fibres that innervates the internal organs and glands, and control the so-called vegetative functions, that is, those functions that are generally beyond voluntary control. The Autonomous Nervous System consists of a "sympathetic modality" that prepares the organism for action / reaction and prepares for the stress reaction, and a "parasympathetic modality" with a stabilising and relaxing function. In the busy everyday life, the sympathetic system prevails. It's not totally negative, it's functional indeed: having a stimulating, exciting, contracting action, it makes our body always ready to defend itself, to fight or flight. In a few moments, the heart increases it's contractile strength and frequency, bronchi, pupils, muscles and the coronary system of blood vessels dilate and all this makes us ready to act. The problem, however, is that in the long run, this hyperactivation causes serious problems and can lead us toward diseases. The Parasympathetic System instead represents the body's normal response to a situation of calm, rest and tranquillity. The parasympathetic mode restores the organism after the stimulation of the sympathetic nervous system. It balances the heart and respiratory rhythm, slows down the pulse, allows a regular blood circulation of all the skin and tissues, helps digestion, manages a correct hormone secretion, lowers blood pressure, increases muscle relaxation: in a word, relaxes. It is this condition, now very rare in everyday life, which can be experienced thanks to Yoga and Meditation. The deep relaxation and breathing of Yoga activates the parasympathetic system, which is responsible for the necessary relaxation reaction if we want to heal our body and mind. Yoga is therefore not a sport, it is not a competition, there is no competition. Those who truly practice Yoga do not see anyone other than themselves.

Yoga teaches the full respect for one's own body and limits, because only those who are able to accept their limits can overcome them. During the lessons we work simultaneously on the physical and mental level, there is no distinction, the breath accompanies every movement and every asana. The asanas are postures and their function, connected to the Indian physiology, is to purify the channels of our body in which the energy flows and, at the same time, they channel this energy towards specific points of our body.

According to Western medicine, the practice of asanas increases strength, flexibility, coordination and balance at the musculoskeletal level.

Asanas are often accompanied by mudras (symbolic gestures of the hands), pranayama (breathing techniques) and mantras (sounds) to enhance their effects. Today there is a great variety of different styles and approaches of yoga, some are pure forms that refer to ancient traditions, whilst others are forms which have been readapted to the Western lifestyle.

Those who suffer from anxiety should prefer "Hatha Yog" lessons whose approach takes into consideration the entirety of the person. Shivananda's Yoga, for example, pays great attention not only to asanas and pranayama (breathing techniques) but also to relaxation, which is done both at the beginning and at the end of the lesson, when the abandonment of the body is accompanied to a vigilant but relaxed mind.

The 4 Asanas against anxiety

Now we present four asanas that can help those who suffer from anxiety
states. For those who are beginners it is essential to follow an expert
teacher and practice Yoga constantly; only in this way they can reach
tangible results. Breathing badly or taking a wrong posture during practice
makes the work you do on yourself totally inefficient.
Also remember that it is always essential not to exceed but to respect the
rhythms and the physical limits. Work gradually within your possibilities.
Every excess is a defect.

1. Balasana – the child. (Bala= child)

This posture aims to improve breathing, calm the nervous system, dissolve the tension accumulated in your back and increase the flexibility of the hips. It's easy to see that it's not advisable for those with knee problems. If you are pregnant, it's good to do it with the legs a little more open and with the arms put forward as a support.

Technique:

1. Start from the quadruped position on your knees and hands.
2. Sit on your heels and slightly open your knees to be in line with your hips.
3. Exhale and lower the torso between your thighs.
4. Place your hands on the floor along your torso with your palms faced up and loosen the front part of the shoulders to the floor (the weight of the shoulders should widen the shoulder blades behind the back).
5. Keep this position for 30 seconds to a few minutes.

2. *Sarvângâsana - the candle. (Sarva = all, whole, complete; Anga = limb or body)*

This asana brings benefit throughout the body. Like all inverted asanas, it tends to lower the heartbeat and slow the breathing. The upside-down position also allows you to see everything from another perspective, thus helping to re-evaluate the importance of things and to recreate a different order. They allow you to develop concentration, memory, they increase self-confidence and reduce the symptoms of anxiety and stress. It must not be performed by people suffering from acute head or neck disease, diseases, thyroid disorders, sinusitis and during the menstrual period. Those suffering from high blood pressure can take this posture only if followed by a teacher. In case of pregnancy it can only be done by experienced practitioners.

Technique:
1. Lie on your back with your legs stretched out, united and stiff, your arms are at your sides with palms facing the ground.
2. Keeping your back firmly on the ground raise your legs bent to your chest.
3. With an exhalation, lift the pelvis from the floor and put your hands on it by bending the arms at the elbows.
4. Exhale and lift the trunk until it is vertical, supporting it with your hands until the chin touches the breastbone. Only the back of the head, of the neck, of the shoulders and back of the arms up to the elbows touch the floor.
5. Exhale and straighten the legs with the tips of the feet facing upward.
6. Maintain the position a minimum of 10 deep breaths.
7. Exhale and lower gradually; free your hands and relax lying flat on the floor.

3. ***Adho Mukha Svanasana - Upside down dog. (Adho mukha = face facing down, Svana = dog)***

When you are tired and exhausted this is the ideal position to relieve fatigue and recover energy. In this position the diaphragm is raised in the thoracic cavity, the speed of the heart beats decreases, the cardiac coherence improves, making us feel more relaxed. It should not be done by those suffering from high blood pressure, carpal tunnel syndrome and from those who have had shoulder or neck trauma. In case of pregnancy it can only be done by experienced practitioners.

Technique:
1. Start from the quadruped position on your knees and hands. Align the wrists under the shoulders and the knees under the hips.

2. During the expiration, pivoting the toes and raise the knees from the ground.

3. Slowly raise the hips   as much as possible and try to lift the tailbone upwards.

4. Stretch out your legs and try to touch the mat with your heels.

5. Push on your hands to move the full body weight on the heels and look at the navel.

6. Hold the position for a minimum of 5 long breaths and then slowly return to the starting position.

4. *Pascimottanasana - Position facing west. (Pascima = west)*

The literal meaning is "Occident" just because in the position there is an intense stretching of the western part of the body. This asana, in fact, acts on the back of the body from the head to the heels. If this is done correctly, this asana massages the heart, the spine and the abdominal organs, as well as to deeply calm the mind. Those suffering from hernias can only perform it under the supervision of an expert teacher.

Technique:
1. Sit on the ground with your legs outstretched and your torso straightened.
2. Exhale and with the help of the hands stretch spine upwards and keeping your spine straight, gradually descend, approaching the stomach to the thighs.
3. Grasp your toes with index and middle fingers.
4. Stretch the spine trying to make the back flat.
5. Exhale, bend and widen the elbows width, using them as levers to touch the knees with your forehead.

6.Keep the asana for at least one minute.

Last and most important advice: always remember to carry out the postures with discipline and consistency because ONLY this way you can see the results you desire so much. Without urgency but also without stopping.

Go, free your energy. Movement is life and life is movement.

*Alice Giusti is an instructor of Yoga, Pilates, Musical Fitness and sport operator for the disabled. After taking courses and updates at the Italian Fitness Federation and the National Educational Sports Centre, she studied Hatha Yoga at the Oriental Academy Satyuga, obtaining the CSEN diploma and the certification of the "Yoga Alliance International". After 10 years of experience in the world of fitness and wellness, in constant personal updating to deepen the issues concerning posture and movement, she works in her studio "MYA", located in Rome, not far from Ponte Milvio.

Chapter 6

Manual of anxiety

6.1 Program 21 steps in 21 days

> *If there's a problem, then there's a solution ...*
> *... and if you want to see the results you must act.*

Finally we move to the part that I love: ACTION. The following is the operating manual to fight anxiety in 21 steps. I know that you won't be able to do all the techniques at once and that's not what I want for you, they are too many, it would only create confusion. The goal is to choose 5 of these techniques and put them into practice every day for 21 days. I recommend you choose the 5 techniques you feel you need the most. After 21 days change your program by choosing new techniques and keeping the ones that work best for you. Always remember that everyone has their strategies and techniques. Focus only on what works for you. Now read them all and mark with a * those you have chosen to put in place from TODAY. Tomorrow is never.

1- Slow down

"Run, run, run, hurry up, there's no time!"

That's what you tell yourself all the time. The problem is something else: by constantly running you don't even know where you are going anymore. You've become a hamster that runs faster and faster, but always on the same wheel. Perhaps you haven't yet noticed that the more you run, the more you are tense and stressed. It's time to say "NO" to everything that accelerates you. Technology continues to invent tools to save time, and all of us are led to invest the moments in an even greater number of activities, with the sole result of not being able to enjoy anything and to feel more and more overwhelmed. If you feel you have also entered this vicious circle, it is time to RESET your speed. Remember that there is no urgency, or rather, there is one: to rebalance your body. To do this you can start with this little exercise of slowing your urgency.

PRESCRIPTION: Choose a daily action that you do in the morning or evening and perform it in **slow motion**. It could be brushing your teeth, making coffee or making your bed, no matter what it is, the important thing is to do it softly and slowly, focusing only on the "here and now" of the action you are doing. This exercise serves to re-educate yourself to find your own rhythm, to stop the state of alarmism, of hurry and anxiety in which we live. It allows you to temporarily loosen the control and to be guided by simple routine actions.

2- Do less

To thrive, it is necessary to do less, make a choice, focus on what is really important, and let go of everything else.

 In this process of eliminating the unnecessary; the harmful and the stressful things, it could be extremely useful to learn to DELEGATE. Doing less and delegating actions radically changes the way you approach life, it means accepting that some situations are beyond your control and that you cannot do everything perfectly on your own.

PRESCRIPTIONS: "If someone points a gun at your head and you are forced to cut 5 of the activities of various kinds that absorb your time, which ones would you eliminate? What are the activities you use to fill the time to feel productive but essentially perpetuate your system of acceleration and stress?"
Learn to ask yourself every day: "if this were the only thing that I will complete today, would I be satisfied with my day?"

Once you have identified the useless actions that fill your time stressing you, eliminate them. Practice in trusting people by delegating some small task, which you generally do, to someone else.

3. **One thing at a time**

   Single-tasking or Multi-tasking? There is no doubt: multi-tasking is just a form of pathological hyperactivity that keeps us running indefinitely without focusing on the real priorities, as well as stressing ourselves. Instead, focusing on one thing at a time will give you greater serenity, the possibility to be the master of your time and of your actions.

   PRESCRIPTION: Force yourself to do only one thing at a time. I know you fear to waste time but by applying this technique you will immediately realise how to do things better and in even less time.

4. Search for the emptiness

Give yourself at least 10 minutes a day in which you "disconnect" from emails, phone calls, messages, TV, radio, etc. Keep some time to put "boundaries" between you and the others, disconnecting yourself from everything. This technique is fundamental both when you need concentration for something important or difficult and to recover balance, energy and focus. Always remaining connected, on the contrary, means being subject to several interruptions and constantly stressed, as well as being always at the mercy of the needs of others. I advise you to practice this exercise before going to sleep, especially if you have difficulty falling asleep or when you feel overwhelmed and not being able to cope with all requests.

PRESCRIPTION: Search for emptiness and be guided by this question: "What do I want?"

Allow yourself a few moments (from 10 to 20 minutes) during the day, of complete emptiness. Visualize the void and let yourself be lulled by the feeling of lightness and tranquillity that inspires you. If you cannot do it, I suggest you gaze at the clouds that move very slowly and keep focused on this image.

Once you have found the image and after fixing your gaze upon it, ask yourself "What do I want in this moment?"

5. Eat slowly

The haste with which we eat is another indicator of the tendency to put ourselves in second place. Nourishing is a gesture of love towards ourselves. Not only does it help you become more satiated and taste the flavours, it is also a way to ease tensions.

PRESCRIPTION: Learn to eat slowly, chew for a long time and enjoy the foods you are eating.

6. Return to the origins

We are made for simple things. Take some time to go out and observe nature. Take inspiration from it, especially to manage your impatience. Remember that nature is not in a hurry, yet everything happens anyway.

PRESCRIPTION: Take some time to go outdoors and observe nature at least three times a week, even better if you do it every day. You can walk, run, and exercise. I suggest you stretch your muscles with simple yoga exercises that you can find on YouTube. And if you do not feel like moving, just sit down and admire the scenery.

My favourite version of this exercise is **WALKING MEDITATION**. It is about walking slowly and coordinating the breathing, not to arrive at a destination, but only to walk. It would be ideal to walk barefoot on the meadow or even on the sand.

Contact with the Earth is an increasingly rare experience today. Yet walking barefoot gives a feeling of widespread well-being. According to Martin Zucker, author of the book *"Earthing"*, barefoot walking helps the connection between the flow of electrical energy of the Earth and our body. In the course of evolution, mankind has walked barefoot and slept on the ground, thus receiving all the benefits of the sweet electric energy of the ground. Walking meditation increases vitality, harmonises and stabilises the basic biological rhythms of the body, reduces chronic inflammation and pain, and, promoting better quality sleep. We can get an immediate energy recharge by simply walking barefoot on a lawn.

7. Rebel against "RULES' TYRANNY"

Delete from your vocabulary the words **"I must"** replace them with **"I can"** or even better replace them with **"I want"**. Replace the word **"guilt"** with **"responsibility"**. Avoid using **"right"** or **"wrong"**.
The dialogue we have with ourselves, the words we use, deeply influence our perception of reality and the behaviours we perform. Every time we use the words "I must" we are forcing ourselves to do something that creates effort, fatigue and stress. Every time we say, "it's right or it's wrong" it's our influences guiding us. Whenever we use the word "guilt", I am labelling someone or something, creating a limiting and rigid reality around us.

PRESCRIPTION: DELETE these words from your life and don't be so hard on yourself. Whenever you use those words remember that you are moving away from your goal.

8. Choose who surrounds you

When you spend time with friends, relatives or acquaintances, you start being "present". You can limit the meetings but when you spend time with them you must "be there" to connect with them, not just meeting them.

Only meet them if you decide not to have your mind busy but the most important thing is that you start to decide who will be a part of your life.

PRESCRIPTION: Choose the people you want in your life. Surround yourself only with those people with whom you feel free to be yourself, they don't judge you and those with positive attitude.

9. Stop Striving

You are not perfect and you will never be. Accept your needs and be indulgent with them. If you feel tired and need to sleep, don't force yourself to stay awake and active. If you need to eat, eat until you feel satisfied. If you need to be alone, do it. If you need to have sex, live your sexuality, find again the desire and the passion. Avoid seeing sex as an obligation, something that "must be done" but only as a pleasure. Awake your sensuality. Live your fantasies, even the most intimate and particular ones.

PRESCRIPTION: During the day admit to yourself, or even better if it's shared with a person you trust, that sometimes you don't feel to be able to live up to some situations. Admitting to having some weaknesses has a **cathartic effect**, it makes us relieved and closer to others. It is the first step to accepting that we are not perfect and to relieve ourselves from our everyday burdens.

10. Recite your Mantra

When you are overwhelmed, maybe even sad and nervous, don't force yourself, you do not have to fight but, on the contrary, you should assume a yielding mental state. It may be helpful to remember a situation that shook or upset you, but this time imagine that you are not trying to fight. You are in a state of passivity, in which you are busy only listening to what is inside of you: your emotions, your feelings and your thoughts. You will immediately realize that what you are experiencing is simply a fluctuating mood and it will pass.

PRESCRIPTION: When sadness, anxiety and frustration are looking for you, stop yourself, breathe and manage your inner dialogue by repeating this mantra three times: *"I have nothing to prove"*.

11. Express Gratitude

Gratitude is one of the personality traits that are the most related to psychological well-being. Gratitude-oriented people are more vital, optimistic and emphatic. Expressing gratitude is the key to live an abundant life full of love.

PRESCRIPTION: Keep a diary and write down every day at least three things for which you are thankful to experiencing.

12. Free yourself

All that is repressed is harmful, try to keep that in mind. You must learn to unleash your emotion, so that nothing of the past is carried into the present. We are full of anger and rancour that block our present and confuse the vision of our future. You can get rid of these repressed emotions in many ways: with a movie or during a conversation, by stopping to pretend that whatever is fine for you. Losing control is a fundamental habit for those who keep everything inside and need to give free rein to emotions, in particular, anger.

PRESCRIPTION: Keep a diary in which you can write everything that comes to your mind, without restraints. Keep it safe. Start by your opinion, when you have opposing opinions to others or when you feel you are facing injustice. Loosen or break some relationships that makes you feel bad, burdened or tired.

13. Learn to say "NO"

Search for your truth, say what you think, avoid holding back your thought, especially if you are facing people who tend to dominate you. Politely refuse if someone asks you too much. You do not have to give explanations, "no" is already a complete answer by itself. Behave according to your code. Do not follow or copy the behaviour of others. Be yourself with your own style. Impose your limits in a firm and healthy way. Others must take responsibility for what happens in their lives. You didn't come into the world to deal with other people's problems. If you allow someone to do whatever they want, you will eventually suffer the consequences. If there are no limits, the relationship is not balanced and doesn't bring benefits. It's not enough to say to yourself that you can no longer stand someone's complaints: you must act.

PRESCRIPTION: Practice in not overloading yourself with responsibilities, problems and commitments just because you don't want to feel guilty. Let go of the guilty conscience. You're not harming anyone. You are just defining your priorities.

14. Disappointing expectations

When you start doing things just because you want to do them, you will immediately realize the reactions or rather the RESISTANCE of the people around you. If they criticise you, if they become cold and unpleasant, it means that you had people who used your accuracy and availability only for their selfish needs. Those who remain, despite your change, are those that accept you for who you are and not for what you do. Disappointing expectations will help you understand who are the clean and healthy people you need to surround yourself with. Don't be afraid of losing someone, put them to the test. Who remains is who loves you; everything else is just a useless waste of energy.

PRESCRIPTION: Everyone expects something from you that now is constricted, it stresses you out and makes you constantly feel unpleasant sensations: it's time to let them down and YOU start dictating the rules of your game. Observe the reactions and you will understand who you are facing.

15. Love

Always remember that the human being loves and nothing makes him happier. We are so busy to achieve the goals, so captured by thousands of things, that we forget that love is the most natural, beautiful and wonderful thing that human beings can live. Love is superior to all our goals because, behind all its activities, the human being is always seeking to love and be loved.

PRESCRIPTION: Ask yourself before going to sleep:
"To who have I given love today?" And " From who have I received love?"

16. Rediscover Pleasure

Engage in a hobby that you have abandoned or, if you've never had one, think of something you'd like to develop. It doesn't matter if you feel capable or not, you will learn, the important thing is that you like it and that it stimulates your creativity. Play, indulge in something fun or silly. Start doing something that in your old way of thinking would be considered "wrong" or a waste of time, but do it just because you want it.

PRESCRIPTION: At least once a week, make or do something you really like, something that excites you. Feel the pleasure in the things you do and feel that you exist: you will understand that there is so much more within you.

17. Stop

When you feel that you are overwhelmed by anxiety, that your thoughts overlap in your head, it is time to stop and reverse the mechanism that would lead you into the vicious circle of anxiety and stress.

PRESCRIPTION: go into the foetal position and bring all the attention on the navel. Begin to breathe and slow down the pace. You will notice that gradually the breath will become homogeneous and at this point, stare at an object and, moving away from all thoughts, wait for the mind to become empty.

18. Meditate

To balance the excessive emotional load, act promptly and meditate for a few minutes. Don't be too demanding, you do not need a place as quiet as church. The important thing is that you are always ready in every place and at every moment to regain balance and to quell the emotions that you don' t want to have.

PRESCRIPTION: Remember that while you are meditating you have to do two things:

1- Breath out to free the negative feelings imprisoned in the body and mind, such as worries and fears; feel them as they vanish every time your lungs are emptied.

2- Lay your hands over your head and see a flow of positive energy descend on you from head to toe.

19. Breathe well

As I explained in the third chapter, practicing diaphragmatic breathing for 5-10 minutes daily helps to calm anxiety, improves health and life. Perhaps you remember that the first thing to do is to understand how you breathe and then correct this breathing method by moving the centre of the breathing lower and lower in the body.
Mastering breathing is essential for healthy self-control.

PRESCRIPTION:

Lie down. Close your eyes. Listen. Empty your mind and focus only on your breathing. Gradually make it slower and deeper.

20. Let yourself go

To let go, to accept uncertainty, to face the fear of the unknown, to loosen the control allow us to understand that there is no threat. You are constantly worried that something bad can happen to you, you are very good at predicting the worst: the problem is that all this tension blocks your present and thus, let yourself go.

PRESCRIPTION: Practice this exercise three times a week. Lie on one side on a soft surface (for example, a Pilates mat) and let yourself loosen. Slowly collapse on your side and stay relaxed for a few moments. Repeat it at least five times with a brief pause between exercises (30 seconds). You will immediately realize that the tension and the resistance is diminished.

21. Now that you know, ACT!

Do you know what's the most powerful prescription? Start the practices immediately. The sooner you start using the techniques and teachings consistently, the more chances you will have of getting rid of anxiety, stress and dissatisfaction. In short, I did everything to share with you everything I know, but now it's your turn.

PRESCRIPTION: take action.

Show the world that you are a tough one, that if you put in your mind one thing, you can complete it and brilliantly.

Now, if you've really decided to change, to abandon the old structure, make a promise to yourself, promise that you'll never again make it easier for passivity and laziness, never again to be persuaded by negativity, but you'll give all of yourself to free your potential and live the life you deserve.

THIS EXERCISE is slightly different from the others because you MUST DO IT EVERYDAY.

There are no excuses, but I'm sure if you've read up to this point, you will do it and you will succeed. I await your email (francescafrascarelli1988@gmail.com) where you tell me that you did it and that you have seen changes, I do not accept excuses!

Conclusions

Here we are at the end. Now it's time to tell you a little secret. During the book I did nothing but feed your anxiety: absurd but it is so. Let me explain. As you may have noticed, I gave you a lot, sometimes too much, information, tasks, exercises and strategies and I pushed you a lot to immediately "put into practice" everything I had taught you. I know that in some moments, during the reading, your anxiety could have been increased, but this is actually my strategy: ***to voluntarily go looking for anxiety.***

Calm down, I'm not crazy, I intentionally did it.

As Viktor Frankl, a noted Austrian psychiatrist, advises:

"Instead of getting rid of anxiety, fear, worries and tensions, we must try to make them grow, to make ourselves feel more anxious, nervous and angry".

That's exactly what I did: the reason I endlessly "battered" you with anxiety is connected to the fact that the more you manage to make the emotions flow, especially the negative ones, the more they will fade.

Matthieu Ricard, a Buddhist monk and scientist, also states:

"The more anger is examined, the faster it will disappear"

By now you have certainly understood perfectly what is the mechanism that fuels anxiety and which defuses it. If this is not the case, I will repeat it again: if you keep avoiding anxiety, it will become stronger and stronger, if you go to seek it voluntarily it vanishes. Only in this way can we stop the escalation of anxiety.

It is not by chance that in an ancient Sumerian tablet we read:

"Look the fear in the face and it will turn into courage, continuously avoid fear and it will turn into panic"

That's the way things are.

Getting free from anxiety is only possible if you first learn to sink into it, to accept it and to dedicate time. Only in this way it will vanish, turning into that excess of vital energy that will profoundly change your life.

Now you really have all the tools you need and when you get a bit of anxiety you will have to do only three things: stop, hug yourself and repeat your personal mantra:

"Everything is alright".

Author
Francesca Maria Frascarelli, Psychologist and health coach.

She deals mainly with energy psychology, paying particular attention to mental and physical imbalances related to anxiety and stress.

Founder of "*Stressologia*", she uses cutting-edge technologies to give customers the best care in a perspective that denies any form of distinction between mind and body.

She believes that mind and body are the same thing and the body can be treated by acting on the mind and, in the same way, heal the mind by acting on the body.
This openness of her mind leads her to devote herself to study and divulgation activities concerning the sphere of "*Extraordinary Healings*".
To find out more, visit the websites:

www.francescafrascarelli.com

www.stressologia.it

The strategies reported in this book are the result of years of studies and specializations and so the achievement of the same results of growth or personal or professional improvement are not guaranteed. The book has exclusively educational and informative purpose. The information contained in this book is not intended to replace the professional opinion of a psychologist and / or physician. The use of any information given here is at the discretion of the reader. The reader assumes full responsibility for his own choices, aware of the risks connected to any form of therapy or exercise. The author is not liable for any direct or indirect responsibility derived from the use or from the application of any indication reported in these pages.

First edition: July 2017
Author: Francesca Maria Frascarelli
Co-author: Giuseppina Pollino
Translation by Elisa Brambilla
Editing by Shannon Doyle

For more updates visit:
www.francescafrascarelli.com
www.stressologia.it

Follow us on FACEBOOK and YOUTUBE:

Dr.ssa Francesca Maria Frascarelli
Dott.ssa Giuseppina Pollino

Bibliography

- *La saggezza dell'anima. Quello che ci rende unici*, Raffaele Morelli, 2016

- *Change Your Brain, Change Your Life*, Daniel G. Amen, 2011
- *La terapia degli attacchi di panico*, Giorgio Nardone, 2016

- *The Code of the Extraordinary Mind*, Vishen Lakhiani, 2017

- *Come Ottenere il Meglio da Sé e dagli Altri*, Anthony Robbins, 2000
- *The Honeymoon Effect. The science of creating Heaven on Earth*, Bruce H. Lipton, 2013

- *The Fear Cure*, Lissa Rankin, 2016
- *Come usare l'enneagramma biologico*, Manuele Baciarelli, 2016

- *The Mind's Own Physician: A Scientific Dialogue with the Dalai Lama on the Healing Power of Meditation*, Jon Kabat-Zinn, Richard J. Davidson, Gyatso Tenzin (Dalai Lama), 2015
- *Con te e senza di te*, Osho, 2009
- *Amore e tantra. Un percorso pratico per la felicità di coppia*, Stefano Ananda, Corienne Ananda,2015
- *Vincere il Panico - Le parole per capirlo - I consigli per affrontarlo - Cosa fare per guarirlo*, Raffaele Morelli, Vittorio Caprioglio, 2016
- *Psicotrappole ovvero le sofferenze che ci costruiamo da soli: imparare a riconoscerle e a combatterle*, Giorgio Nardone, 2013

- *The Soul's Code: In Search of Character and Calling*, James Hillman, 2009
- *Dieta e Ormoni per la salute del seno*, Gianluca Pazzaglia con Francesca Frascarelli, 2016

- *L' ormone della salute*, Gianluca Pazzaglia con Francesca Frasacarelli, 2017